EMPOWERMENT

Blending Ageless Wisdom
into Modern-Day Life

Phil Murray

Hodder & Stoughton

First published in 1995 by Perfect Words and Music
Published in 1999 by Hodder and Stoughton
A division of Hodder Headline PLC

10 9 8 7 6 5 4 3 2 1

British Library Cataloguing in Publication Data

A CIP catalogue record for this title is available from the British Library.

ISBN 0 340 71791 2

Printed and bound in Great Britain by
Mackays of Chatham plc, Chatham, Kent

Hodder and Stoughton
A division of Hodder Headline PLC
338 Euston Road
London NW1 3BH

This book is dedicated to
Advanced PAC Practitioners

Just as a pebble thrown onto still water produces ripples;
so too does the constant affirmation of the positive affect the negative.
The vibration of this phenomenon is a service to humanity and individual alike!

the plan

Key to Symbols

✎   refers to a written exercise

✿   suggests illumination through pondering

🏃   means *get the concept into action*

𝄞   play your favourite instrumental music in
the background

SK   denotes comment by a Silent Knight
*a Silent Knight is a person who unselfishly
flows mental love and forgiveness into the
world for the benefit of all!*

Introduction

It can be tempting to skip introductions and forewords in books, as it is so often the case that they are irrelevant, long winded, dull, boring and not written by the author whose book you have just purchased. It is sometimes an attempt also, to get straight to the point of securing the knowledge promised by the work.

This book is different!

It is a revelation of the essence contained in *all* true religions, and now released in this volume as a practical guide to personal success. If you are looking for shames, guilts, sacrifices, rigid holy disciplines and help with repentance, replace this book on the shelf if you are browsing in a bookstore, it will not help unless you are willing to change your approach to achievement.

I treat personal development as a celebration!

No further commitment will be required by you the reader, to relinquish control on any aspect of your life as an exchange for this information. You don't have to *join up*, and I have no intention of burdening the world with another cult or sect that believes it's way is the only way! Ageless Wisdom predates and transcends the teachings of all known religions; I have therefore utilised in the main, paragons and aspirations from this body of knowledge, which I hold to be the root of all divine knowledge that man is capable of knowing, with the exception of a senior authority which can only be found in each and every one of us ... The God Within!

A letter is included towards the rear of the book, which was sent to me by a friend who calls himself a *Silent Knight*, and asks to remain anonymous. I respect this wish, and request that you read this letter first, only if you promise that its complicated and advanced viewpoints, will not be off putting to your continuing with the reading of this book, which has been written with the gradient scale of acceptance anchored to the forefront of my mind, and you the reader firmly visualised by me in a relevant context.

Otherwise, read this letter last of all, by which time it will sit more congruently within your own general understanding of life.

Read the whole book from beginning to end, then read it again and make its contents a part of your operating basis. Get into action with the theory introduced to you herein ... this presentation has already begun!

There are many words used that are perhaps new to you. If they do not form part of your regular vocabulary, you will need to involve yourself in some dictionary work. Make sure you understand all of the words ... in so doing you will open up new concepts previously veiled through an insufficient word-stock. Part of the potency imparted to you by this book is an increased mental lexicon. Word power *becomes* understanding! New concepts are communicated by words. Even though language is insufficient to transmit the grander concepts of ageless wisdom, it is a tool which we must use ... and make of it the best we can!

Nothing seems strange to me anymore ...too many coincidences have led me away from such a concept, to that of telepathy and cosmic consciousness. If I could give you one quick fix right here and now, it would be this ... *give!* Yet the popular concept within the world of personal development is *ask the world what you want of it, and the world will do its best to give it to you!* This is also a concept which I utilise, yet I know it to be an inferior relation to the simple outflow of giving. We are human however, and this book deals with real issues, not just starry eyed solutions that flow poetically onto the paper.

It could take some time, but the mental creations of today, are the physical manifestations of tomorrow. I therefore advise you to *think the right thoughts* ...

The mental beginnings of this book included the possibility of composing it as a writing triangle ... three separate writers in three different locations ... communicating by modem, floppy disc and telephone; together with the tuning of minds to a particular focus which would inevitably lead to a degree of telepathy.

I had two other writers in mind ... one lady in Europe and one gentleman living elsewhere. The first connection did not work out, and I had to relegate that experience to the realms of *physical universe limitations*. My other friend however, who calls himself a *Silent Knight*, not only agreed to contribute, but enriched my experience with factual data that could only be accrued through time spent on this planet and good intentions. I reciprocated his flow with a sharing of my artistic influence, made possible only through my years in the world of entertainment; he also benefitted from my enthusiasm and direction.

As the triangle was created in my mind, so did its actual physical existence have to occur, and I was premature only in detail. Through the Positive Attitude Club connection, Dani Humberstone agreed to illustrate the ideas with her own artistic interpretations. Dani runs a successful greeting card publishing company; I received one of her creations through the post and immediately enquired as to her availability. The result of these relationships is splendid ... this book!

Interdependence is not about dictating ideas to colleagues ... it is about introducing a concept and arriving at a mutually beneficial conclusion; in the case of this work, for readers also. Consequently, I have written the book; the less than Silent Knight has contributed in a way which still deprives me from the right to state his name, and the illustrations are by Dani.

We all hope that you thoroughly enjoy this interdependent venture, and find a place in your life for the ageless wisdom that has undoubtedly touched ours ...

With love from the triangle ... ▲

Foreword

are we blessed or cursed and if either, by what?

Planetary Involution for what we now call Human Being was a long process. In fact it was the same length as Evolution for this particular universal time period *will* be. The act of becoming involved with this material world was a spiral downward through many different phases, from a spirituality biased existence of togetherness, to that in which we now find ourselves emersed. The peak of solidity is now behind many of us, and we have begun to embrace higher ideals and some finer aspects of existence. Faster vibrations are now available to Humanity, making the contemplation of our next developmental step possible, and as a species it would be incredibly expeditious if we were able to reach a group decision on just how quickly we should target the tuning of an ability to touch this new dimension which is coming into play.

Of course, we are all at different stages of Evolution both within and without this new upturn of the spiral; as has been the case throughout cosmic existence, each person's introduction to stimulation from and response to this new energy, will appear at different times, sometimes even ahead of those who apparently are even more worthy of this favour.

We became involved, to gain experience of self awareness ... to grasp an understanding of individuality ... to feel separateness and reach full perception of the physical plane. We needed pain, sorrow, suffering and sacrifice in order to reach the bottom of the spiral ... selfishness was necessary as a precursor to altruism ... suspicion and exclusiveness were harnessed in order to appreciate inclusiveness, and love without ulterior motive.

... these ideas partly constitute a Cosmic Plan which I sense

11

with greater ease as time goes by. I strive to understand and experiment ... with each new day comes a deeper understanding ... with this fresh enlightenment I strive to maintain a useful relationship and practical connection to the physical world ... the business ... the house ... the Family ... the friends ...

I pondered the title of this Foreword and conclude that **we were blessed with a curse by The Friendliest Force.** A simplistic answer which serves me well. With our new experience we must now evolve away and upward from this nadir, and indeed many people sense that such a process has already begun to happen.

One cannot become involved with personal development research honestly, without touching on vital questions connected to Cosmic Existence. When looking for answers to questions posed by people *trying to get what they want from this life,* research demands to know how similar aspirations can be or have been achieved elsewhere.

For me, the **Hermetic Axiom ...** *"As above, so below; as below, so above,"* from **The Kybalion**, is a practical tool. This Principle, or *Law of Correspondence*, enables a glimpse of Life's aspects which could not be otherwise contemplated.

In order to compose personal development data for the utilisation of those seeking to improve on what they already are, it is essential to be cognisant of bigger and broader axioms. To avoid this necessity would result in the steering of readers towards small minded targets and aspirations; including perhaps, a rehashed well worn route which the self help industry still uses ... the focusing on tricks of the trade like *how to get someone to buy when they don't really need what you are selling.* That is not personal development! It is a form of inter personal rivalry which is obsolete as a modus operandi with all but the most backward of peoples! The types of

12

philosophical concepts which are discussed during the dissemination of such work however, are quite easily absorbed by the majority of *new horizon seekers*, and confusion sometimes arises between ease of assimilation and usefulness. In order to proceed beyond what has now become the norm, which I loosely describe as work begun in the last century by authors like the Englishman James Allen; to the beginning of the twentieth century by Henry Thomas Hamblin; continued in the middle of this century by Napoleon Hill, W Clement Stone, Claude Bristol and Harold Sherman; up to this day when we have an abundance of opinion and technique from people such as Anthony Robbins, Brian Tracy, Stephen Covey, Wayne Dyer, Shad Helmstetter, Dennis Waitley, Shakti Gawain and many others, we must tolerate the transient reference to higher teachings, which may not be appealing in their purest form to the vast majority of personal development students; it will however, become apparent as one loosens a grip on any bigotry and intolerance that may lurk within, that such reference is invaluable.

Just as the Sun's rays could prove lethal to Mother Earth if exposure to them was inordinately extensive; night time arrives and brings with it the Moon, which reflects those same rays onto our Planet, after sapping some of the power which would have constituted the mortal blow ... *so this work is in the line of just such reflective service*.

It is a sacrilege to alter even the smallest nuance of *The Great Universal Teachings*; just as it is treacherous to mankind when the utilisation of technology such as that obtained through atomic discoveries, results in death and destruction. The main reason why such Great Universal Teachings of The Ageless Wisdom remain esoteric, is that most people are unable to distinguish right from wrong. Even when the differentiation has been made, the act that follows is often in direct contradiction to the conclusion reached. Because of this, many powerful Universal Laws are hidden from the majority, or coded in such an exoteric fashion as to deem them impotent. The Bible is an example of work that contains many secrets available esoterically to some, whilst retaining full exoteric readability for those not yet in possession of the key to its coded riddles.

Your ability to utilise any techniques that this volume will make available to you, relates in direct proportion to your purity of purpose. Mark these words well, and constantly check both your aspirations and actions for integrity; let it be known that ignorance or temporary contamination of your intention, holds no sway with the superficially simple Law of Karma.

What you give *is* what you will get; for the foreseeable future it will never ever be any other way.

Most personal development data is focused on *Personality* ... my work is centred around *Character*. I align *Personality* with *Historical Planetary Involution*, and *Character* with *Unfolding Universal Evolution*. This is why the Positive Attitude Club, about which more information will be available as we progress, does not concern itself with learning how to smile for the furtherance of purely selfish desires ... rather ... the bias is wholly in favour of true development from within.

We can already be *Personality* ... so now we must evolve an understanding and utilisation of *Character*. I therefore further align *Personality* and *Historical Planetary Involution* with *the Material World*; then *Character* and *Unfolding Universal Evolution* with *the Spiritual Macrocosm*.

Through approaching Personal Development from this angle I am aware potentially of an imminent departure for my work from the mainstream shelves in the book stores, and if that happens then so be it. I am confident that such policy would be transient, as

14

more and more people sicken of the quick fix and begin a creative endeavour towards discovery of the true self. This outlook of mine is also a privilege of owning ones own publishing company ... I am not chained to an editor's restraining viewpoint. My conscience has replaced the need for such a person. Nor am I attracted to the *follow up strategy*, which is an analogy from the music business and certainly current *popular publishing speak*.

My first book entitled *You Can Always Get What You Want*, was a natural introduction of my values and techniques, synthesised from a variety of sources and catalysed into a working formula, then introduced into the world of Personal Development. It stands as an inspirational work and will continue to be useful for many years to come. It was apparent to me, as I emersed myself in research, that it was relatively easy to *Get What You Want* from life, yet far more challenging and rewarding to find the *Win For All Ingredient* mentioned especially in Stage Six of *You Can Always Get What You Want*, as an altruistic assault on old value systems and Piscean solidity.

This thinking led me to write my second book which is called *Before the Beginning is a Thought*. This work is a statement of belief in the Cosmos being a mental creation. It suggests that any challenges encountered during regular human existence, should be confronted utilising our ever more apparent mental faculties, which will grow in power much as an athlete's muscles do through training.

I began the Positive Attitude Club in the first book, as a way of transmitting certain information on a light carrier wave. Learners became PAC, pronounced PACK People, who then graduated as PAC Practitioners. When enough knowledge was achieved, they were self promoted to the grade of Advanced PAC Practitioner. Maintaining the sixth sense of humour firmly to the forefront of my contemplations, I became Leader of the PAC, and the idea maintained a light and serviceable impression of personal development data. I continued the concept to a lesser degree in the second book, and as the PAC became a growing physical organisation, so did my observation that much talk was easy, but practical applications were scarcer, yet more valuable.

Thus, I maintain the PAC in pride of place, as a concept which will underpin this new book. Perhaps *Positive Action Club* would bear a greater relationship to the role which the organisation in this current work will take, but I shall leave the PAC as it is ... an *attitude* club ... I leave the name, and your transmutation of *attitude* into *action* for individual analysis.

My impulse is towards progress, and the Positive Attitude Club is an intimate cell of a personal whole which I tend and nurture for many reasons. As long as the PAC remains useful to its members and adherents, then so will its life continue to flourish. Its Service is to **The Friendliest Force!**

Whoever .... Wherever ... Whenever.

I am aware of an abundance of words written about Life, the Cosmos, Spirituality, Self Improvement and the striving for refinement as human beings. I am not aware of as many practical guides which concentrate on putting those words into action. This word *action* is a key expression within the formula for success in this world, or indeed any other world that I can presently conceive of. We may well be motivating in the direction of a more concentrated mental approach to life, but it is with *action* that such an operating basis will prove fruitful ... whether this action is mental or physical will depend on requirements of individual situations. There is a great divide between PAC members and PAC Practitioners; and then a further chasm exists as one challenges the barriers frequently experienced on a journey towards Advanced PAC Practitionership.

Thinking Positively is an important step, but only if the impulse is towards Acting Positively; and only then if such contemplations and actions are undertaken with a comprehension of the Greater Whole ... **The Friendliest Force, which is LO♡E.**

I now offer you Empowerment

Phil Murray
15th of April, 1995

getting to know you

Guide One

getting to know you

Because a man prays long and loud is not a sign that he is a saint ... *chapter 101 verse 19, The Aquarian Gospel of Jesus the Christ by Levi.*

Alignment of purpose

I begin this personal development book on an intimate note quite deliberately, and with a practical strategy firmly in mind. *Getting to know you* is a cliché when it refers to someone else, but when this well worn phrase is redirected at the self it takes on a freshness of meaning.

The written word has grave limitations when utilised to discuss grander concepts. In fact, until one is able to contemplate beyond the verbal language, it will be evident that severe restrictions challenge any reach for true personal success. We have however, a communication challenge ahead of us which will utilise the medium of written words, and with these restrictions acknowledged we can continue on the understanding that your inner feelings about all of the subject matter which we shall discuss in this work, will always take precedence over any viewpoints that I have to offer you.

Let me ask you some questions.

Who are you? What are you? Where are you? How are you?

Perhaps more important a question is *when are you?*

Do not think too deeply about these points as yet; just get acquainted with the flavour of the approach that we are making to personal development ... taste the questions as you would a dish freshly created from a new recipe.

If you are the type of person who appreciates the potency invoked through the writing down of thoughts physically onto paper, then I suggest you *begin with the end in mind*, as Dr Stephen Covey plainly puts it in his excellent book entitled *The Seven Habits of Highly Effective People*. You can prod this sentiment into action by equipping yourself with a pen or pencil and some suitable writing material, preferably a good quality notepad which you can keep alongside the book; this is a practical manual of applications and the *end* which I suggest *you* should have in mind is **Self Empowerment**.

The definition that I apply to the title of this book comes from the *New College Edition of the Heritage Illustrated Dictionary of the English Language, International Edition*. It describes the word as meaning: *1. To invest with legal power; authorize. 2 To enable or permit.*

The word *legal* I further qualify for our mission as meaning ethical, moral and in keeping with a general code of conduct not directed by the law, but felt from within as being beneficial to humanity as well as yourself. The word *enable*, I suggest can apply to a power within you which is already in existence, but lying dormant, waiting for you to crack the code. *Permit*, I direct at your giving of permission for your latent powers to manifest in their full glory.

Do our definitions of the word agree for all practical purposes?

If you want the word to mean *kicking into play Personality Power*, then I am afraid this book will be of little use to you, until that is, you are more pliable in your pondering of the word *achievement*, with the adjective *true* restraining it.

True achievement is that which you are able to take with you when you finish with this life and progress on your evolutionary way.

The first exercise I would like to involve you with is this:

Write the word *Empowerment* at the top of your first page
in large print, then beneath it, define the word thoroughly
to your satisfaction and complete comprehension.

Word power is a crucial ingredient of full power. For the
intellect, words are the keys to new concepts, much as symbols
give a more holistic understanding of ideas in an intuitive way,
only to a lesser degree. You may find that your definition of this
word is at variance with the one which I am utilising. If this is so,
then you must ask yourself if it is close enough for the information
that I shall impart to be effective in your life, and then answer
yourself honestly.

You now have the definition of your *Empowerment* aspiration
written out for reference; if that is, you have decided to *practice*
these exercises ... an action which I thoroughly recommend. You
can refer to it, throughout your study of this material as a reminder
of direction. Each time your definition adopts a fresh nuance of
meaning, then so must you redefine it in writing, thus illustrating
your progress.

Illuminate the word through the action of pondering.
Contemplate enable, and if it is not already in your
definition, should it be?

Rediscover one attribute of your character that you do not
ever utilise ... enable it and empower yourself with its
qualities. Remember that this is an activity which you need

21

to actually physically practice. If for instance, you rediscover your communication power to make people feel good about themselves, then you must go out into the field and exercise this ability with a thorough workout. Utilise the initial burst of energy that you will experience after the mental cognition, and get into action as quick as is practically possible in your particular circumstances.

Who are you?

Do you know? You have been with the personality known as *you* for quite some time now ... it is an easy mistake to confuse identities! Or is it?

You don't *be a car* just because you ride in it. You are not crazy if you visit someone in a mental institution. Do you assume the identity of a Dickensian character after buying a Victorian property? Are you old because you live in a Georgian house?

SK

This is a subject we have often discussed Phil ... *YOU ARE NOT WHAT YOU HAVE!* When you say *my* car, *my* name, or *my* hand ... *my* denotes possession or ownership by someone ...YOU! So when you say *my* name, *my* body, *my* mind, *my* Soul, *my* Spirit ... keep a thought on who(m) or what *has* these *things*, and you will have the *OWNER*. All that will be left is I AM! That is The Owner. This is best done in contemplation during meditation, or what you call TTM. This is precisely the most simple path to self-realization taught by Ramana Maharshi, known by many in India as the *Last of the Great Living Saints*.
... *end of note.*

Of course not; and neither are *you* your body! You need a form with which to experience this physical universe and your body is just that. A vehicle which you must respect, and a tool which is essential for the gathering of evolutionary experience hinted at in the Foreword. This body was born with inherent features which can be easily compared with other members of your immediate Family, and even more distant relatives. What is it that provides the spark which allows this body to think and behave individually?

You!

The Human Being is in the vanguard of this particular wave of evolution, having achieved *individual* consciousness. An animal has consciousness too, but it is group awareness manifested by a collective spirit. Lower down the chain we find the plant and then the mineral kingdoms. The consciousness is less, like a dreamless sleep in the case of plants, the lower one descends down the line.

Charles Darwin's *Theory of Evolution*, which unfortunately is now accepted without inspired thought by much of western civilisation, was never an holistically convincing part of my historical reflections. In order to take your studies of this very relevant subject of history and future development further, you could examine work already accomplished by Max Heindel, in, *The Rosicrucian Cosmo-Conception*. This is an extremely easy book to read even though it deals with human spirituality in great depth. It is not the role of this book on *Empowerment*, or its Author, to reveal information which is already available in a very pure form and written by a person of far greater expertise.

ﾗ

If this Max Heindel book is part of your requirements, then now is the time to note down its title and order it.

The earliest authoritative work that I know to be in existence which deals with the subject of Involution and Evolution is HP Blavatsky's, *The Secret Doctrine*, which I would describe as a comprehensive and masterly reference which inspired many books that were to follow, perhaps even the one already mentioned. *The Secret Doctrine* is in two volumes and will need thorough

23

commitment if you choose to study it ... the benefits are however, lasting, and any initial endeavour will be rewarded in a practical fashion through reflection into your life of certain principles, which are planetary axioms not readily found in modern personal development literature.

Who you are is essential to know for one simple reason ... you need to be cognisant of the answer before knowing how to treat yourself. You wouldn't expect a petrol engine to perform well on a heavier fuel oil would you? Would a tiger survive on the diet of a rabbit? No! So it is with you.

You have a body which could possibly survive much as does an animal, if the indwelling spirit was not active. This can be viewed by considering examples of people from where you consider to be the top end of the spiritual scale, the middle, and then the bottom.

At the top in band one, you will find people who place ideals and non tangible concepts at the very doorway to all that they hold precious in this world. It would be improbable if you were ever able to make them an offer they could not refuse, if that offer meant compromising any scrupulous objective that they were working towards.

In the middle, called band two, which is the fastest growing sample, you will find a group populated by those members of Humanity currently experiencing an equilibrium between Spirit and Matter. Friction is created between the two opposing features. Here, the lower mind will be evident, but a qualifying force of spirit will be felt increasingly, in direct proportion to the amount of goodwill exerted by the specific Being. Examples of this phenomenon are ... wanting to hit someone and stopping yourself ... wanting a possession that one cannot afford, having an opportunity to steal it, but refusing to seize such chance ... an impulse to criticise halted by the knowledge of the potential damage.

At the bottom end of the scale in band three, can be seen the dismal examples of our races. People unwilling to take responsibility for their own lives let alone others. This sample are the easiest to sway in opinion and are frequently abused as such through advertising and rumour mongering. They recite the latest tabloid headline as if it is one of life's precious maxims. They often feel *badly done to*, yet act feebly to change their circumstances. They are following the instincts of the lower mind, which is only marginally more capable than that of an advanced animal, yet lacking in many aspects of instinct, which is much more evident in all animals. This is a dangerous situation which affords such people similar rights to those more environmentally responsible. This sample require direction, but more importantly, a flow of love and acknowledgement for all that they accomplish in the direction of their spiritual instincts, and each conquest over their lower impulses. This band is indeed the most heavily populated. Fortunately, the fastest growing band already mentioned is the one directly above this lowest sample, and consequently fed in ascension from it. It is the exception, that falls from the top to the middle; I know of none and for this fact we should be thankful.

So, who are you? You are a spiritual being dwelling in a body which you have become identified with. If this was not the case, then you would not experience any qualifying force over basic, lower mind desires. This force is spirit. You. The *I Am* which a Silent Knight has already mentioned. As the fundamental impulse is towards progress, then it is evident that identification with the spiritual side of yourself is somewhat more desirable than the alternative, of living at the whim of the lower mind and baser instincts.

What are you?

The answer is dependent on the implementation of your desires. It is related to the three categories of Humanity already mentioned, and takes into account the personality which will be engaged in some activity on the physical plane to make human survival possible. Are you just personality? This will be evident by your ability to divert purely selfish aims to more altruistic endeavours. Epitomes of the personality syndrome are often parodied in television and film. The smiling TV presenter who scowls and shouts the moment the camera is no longer focused on him. Preachers and Ministers who extol the virtues of the great prophets, yet engage in conduct little tolerated throughout what I have described as band three of Humanity. The politician who supports an Act of Parliament dedicated to cleansing the streets from vice, yet actively practicing sexual perversions he or she has pledged to oppose.

What you are is dependent on what you think you are ...
in action!

The sum total of everything you think in its physical manifestation is exactly what you are. You cannot hide what you are from a trained observer, or even a casual onlooker from a higher band. The evidence of your most private thoughts are apparent to such people. As you ascend the spiritual scale, you will discover more and more that it is your thoughts which are the focus of true personal development. These contemplations are the immediate precursors to any physical manifestation you will bring into being for all to see, hear and experience.

What you are is physically visible all around you!

Where are you?

Planet Earth is on the upturn of a spiral proceeding towards a pre-ordained future. One of the most beneficial paradoxes I have ever personally grappled with, is the fact that there is a Divine Plan, yet each and every human being amongst us has the right and ability to exert individual free will. What is the Plan? It is a concept with which you must personally work, and become sensitive to. The more we are able to co-operate with the cyclical nature of this Planet, and tune in to the faster vibrating frequencies, the sooner we will enjoy the fruits of this endeavour in the form of living in the light with our own positive aspirations.

This planet that we call home, is a living breathing entity. You are a cell in this body we call Mother Earth, just as a cell on the end of your little finger is part of you. Earth is part of a greater macrocosm experiencing its own evolutionary process. Your location on this planet exposes you to certain energies ... it is manipulation and utilisation of such phenomena that will set you apart from the rest and give your own process an impetus so far only dreamt about. You are in a group of people called Humanity ... *The One Life* ... together with all the rest of us. Countries, divisions and sub divisions pale into insignificance when viewing the *Big Picture*. Advanced PAC Practitioners always view this big picture as an essential to understanding.

So, where you are is dependent on where you think you are ... *thoughts are things* ... you must decide on the feasibility of believing in the *Oneness of Humanity*, and if you do, then that is where you are ... at one with your fellow man and surroundings.

How are you?
PAC Learners believe in Life. PAC People believe in nurturing an ability to be at cause over life. PAC Practitioners enjoy the experience of making things happen. Advanced PAC Practitioners understand life and the significance of philanthropy. These descriptions illustrate ascending states on the PAC Ladder.

Most of us are born into a family where it is relatively easy to

27

assume the title of PAC Learner. Some are not however, and spend a lifetime of friction announcing all that cannot be accomplished ... then going on to try and achieve just that which has been deemed impossible by none other than themselves. This book is not for such people, as they must spend a lifetime or more learning from experience that *before each beginning is a thought*; then they will progress upward to trial and error, before realising that nobody can afford the punishment of a negative thought, and other such non directional motivations. The Positive Attitude Club begins its endeavours with those of us known as Learners. These people have acknowledged that there is something to learn which could make their lives a little easier, and certainly more productive. How are they? They are this advantageous way because they have acknowledged the spark within, and then demanded their right to learn.

PAC People are apparent because of their constant affirmation which can manifest in the telling of others to *think positively*. It is a type of lip service eminently more beneficial than living life as it is dished out. They remain at this foundational stage, because they have not taken the aspirational plunge into unknown waters, where action according to their theory could prove them wrong; this possibility they have no wish to confront. Pride is an obstacle yet to be overcome. They mainly live within a verbal casing of wordy platitudes and talk of possibilities which occasionally manifest into being, often much to their own amazement.

PAC Practitioners are exactly as their title suggests ... *in action* ... the best state to be in when an idea has been formulated and an aspiration acknowledged. You can find such people busy in every social strata of society. The British and American Yuppie of the 1980's typified one angle of such people, *upwardly mobile* being the operative part of that partial acronym; but it would be myopic of me and misleading to you if I were not to outline the many other aspects visible in such members of the Positive Attitude Club.

Giving is an acknowledged attribute of theirs. The processing of negative feedback to gain advantage is a quality they also possess. The flowering of a tendency to listen and understand others is thankfully blatant. Achievement is an expected episode in their lives, and a faint understanding of the *Oneness* begins to make inroads into their working environment.

Advanced PAC Practitioners have the ability to do nothing, just as they have full knowledge of the moment when it is necessary to get into speedy action. They are not dictated to by news headlines or the latest opinion making its rounds on the grapevine. Gossip has been expelled from their lives, if it was ever there in the first place, and a positive commitment to non critical communication has taken its place. Advanced PAC Practitioners have transcended the need for instant material gratification and can quite happily exist on their inner achievement in mental matter, fully knowing that it is only a question of time before their thoughts find tangible expression on the physical plane, viewable by the masses. This is a comfortable level of achievement, rendered uneasy only by the fact that it is ever more apparent that *the more you know, the more you know there is to know.*

A reminder at this point in the book, that the Positive Attitude Club is both a physical reality, and a concept that you can carry with you at all times; or as and when required. It is not a sect or cult. This book is utilising the PAC for both analogous and actual examples relevant to personal development.

How are you can only be answered by yourself. You are a certain way because you have gone into agreement with particular traits which have been displayed by others, or offered to you by your own lower instincts or higher spiritual beingness. I offer you these definitions of PAC States in the hope that you will honestly pinpoint yourself on the ladder and aspire towards ascension. For those who acknowledge its existence, the path of personal development is there for all to tread. Half way along its length another Path comes into view. This Path is spiritual in nature, and will form a solid walkway for all who aspire towards true greatness. The Advanced PAC Practitioner has a foot on each Path and a choice to constantly effect. Such advanced state allows a glimpse of more evolved aspirations, but a firm choice has to be made in order for the transfer between Paths to be smooth and complete. One path is material in essence, and the other Path is spiritual in its entirety.

The spiritual Path can be disruptive to an average everyday type life ... constant challenges are made to human equilibrium, and at times, ostensible sacrifice of certain personal development path traits can be necessary. The PAC stands at that point where both paths can be seen, and part of its purpose is to facilitate an easy transition between the two. Modern spirituality will be demonstrated in the workplace, on the streets and in the public bars of every western city. It will find its way into the lives of both *the haves* and *have nots*, alike. It acknowledges the need for both leaders and followers, sitting in judgement on neither; thus, it embraces both leadership and followership as necessary branches of the same eventuality.

The ascetics of history are the executives of the now. The monks of Holy Orders who sat guarding the lesser secrets of White Magic lest such formulae be discovered and used for black and dishonourable purpose, will be replaced by the personal development teachers of the present day working in the field, who have become sensitive to the need for an accelerated progress towards true personal success, which they understand must ultimately be spiritual. The lesser mysteries of the Ageless Wisdom will fall more and more into their hands, as and when they display an ability to share powerful formulae with minds which are ready to utilise such knowledge for unselfish gain.

You are how you are through choice!

When are you?

... on those occasions when you feel the vibrancy of present time and the potency of your own power! You know that you are not trying to be like anyone else ... not thinking like the last book you have just read without having assimilated the data and made it your own ... a satisfaction of your situation is apparent, even though you will strive for positive change ... tolerance of others is easier even though personal tastes remain the same ... more of you is evident when you find your responses quicken ... communication lags, caused because of the channelling of a question through what you consider to be someone elses more authoritative viewpoint cease, and you feel a freedom to wander around your own perspective fully cognisant of the simple fact that you are the best person to handle whatever situation you are in. When are you? You are more you as you allow more of you to percolate through the veils and shadows that you may or may not have created to mask your beingness, for fear of being hurt!

Make a list of traits that are knowingly demonstrated by you on a daily basis, and pinpoint yourself on the PAC Ladder. Define the word ascension in writing, using any references to Christ as analogous only.

Illuminate a concept by pondering the word ascension, and any connotations this word may bring into your mind. Does its definition include the ideas of challenge; the overcoming of undesirable instincts; the climbing above lesser states to reach loftier plateaux?

Rise above your present attributes and decide to allow even greater qualities to come into your life. Pinpoint a trait just

31

above your position on the PAC Ladder and demonstrate this characteristic as a personal attribute. Remember this is an exercise involving *action*.

May I stress that the human categories and descriptions that I have mentioned thus far in the book, involve no judgement or condescending tolerance of others on my part; I propose that you should utilise such dry information for your own internal guidance only. The dangers of summing a fellow human being up succinctly in a few platitudinous words should already be evident to you from your own experience of life. If you feel yourself rising above those around you in an arrogant and judgmental fashion, then it is wise to have a mental tool ever ready for your escape from such emergencies.

Let me share with you, a poem written by an old lady in a geriatric ward of a London Hospital. It was found in her locker after she died, by staff who thought her incapable of writing.

Beneath the Skin

What do you see nurse, what do you see?
What are you thinking when you look at me,
A crabbit old woman, not very wise.
Uncertain of habit with far away eyes.
Who dribbles her food and makes no reply
When you say in a loud voice "I do wish you'd try."
I'll tell you who I am as I sit here so still
As I rise at your bidding, as I eat at your will.
I'm a child of ten with a father and mother
Brothers and sisters who love one another.
A bride soon at twenty my heart gives a leap
At twenty five now I have young of my own
Who need me to build a secure happy home
At fifty once more babies play around my knee
Again we know children my loved one and me

Dark days are upon me my husband is dead.
I look to the future I shudder with dread,
My young ones are busy rearing young of their own
And I think of the years and the love I have known
I'm an old woman now and nature is cruel
Tis her jest to make old age look like a fool
The body it crumples, grace and vigour depart
There is a stone where I once had a heart
But inside this old carcass a young girl still dwells
And now and again my battered heart swells.
I remember the joys, I remember the pain
And I'm loving the living all over again
And I think of the years all too few, gone too fast
And I accept the stark fact that nothing will last
So open your eyes nurse, open and see
Not a crabbit old woman, look close and see me.

TTM ... time to myself

I know from running the PAC that around about 50% of those who attend physical Gatherings, do not practice any kind of mind control on themselves. At the end of the evening we usually mentally exercise ourselves with a varied meditation, and close with *The Great Invocation*, as a service to both ourselves and others. One particular evening as we began, I suggested that everyone empty their heads of all thoughts and emotions. A new PAC Person stated that this was impossible ... *the shopping list ... things to do tomorrow ... the kids birthday present* ... these were the type of things that she mentioned were constantly going through her mind, and of course she assumed such was the case for everyone else. It was a real help to the whole PAC that she spoke about this supposition, because it was apparent that she was not the only one with this mental challenge ahead of her. Also it is part of the PAC purpose to help with such matters.

Firstly, the concept was alien. This person had not ever

considered that such mastery was possible. Secondly, if such was the case then how could it be accomplished and why?

The opposite of personal mind control is mental anarchy. If you allow this state of affairs to exist in your cerebral universe then you are the effect of these stray thoughts. They serve no useful purpose, and strangle any stillness that could exist as a medium for creativity. The mind is a tool which places you at the base of the very pinnacle of evolution, yet still not much is really known about the possibilities of mind manipulation. Certain unscrupulous individuals have harnessed specifically crude methods for the furtherance of personal goals, or their country's aims; this has introduced fear of the unknown into the equation for many. Parlour psychology has proved a useful tool for the degradation of mind understanding; this has been many a naive person's first and last experience of looking inward. Clinical psychology has served us no better. Some cults are cognisant of mind power and utilise it as bait. The offer from such organisations is often connected to *personal power* achievement, a state which is rarely achieved by unscrupulous methods. When acquired by the few however, it is often then turned against them in an effort to keep their wallets attached to the group. Those attracted by the temptation of non substantial self aggrandisement, are particularly targeted by sects and cults; they are however not the only ones to fall under the spell; this frightens people from becoming involved in any organisation involved with mental processes no matter how loose that involvement may be. Drugs had a negative effect on the subject, and mind contorting substances are now available as an important leisure component and accessory for all occasions ... so the pushers would have you believe!

It would do no one any good at all if there was a magic button which could be pushed to reveal all ... tempting though that prospect might appear. We are here to gain experience ... if one was able to pop an LSD tab and see all, then that would be the

34

experience ... popping the tab! Stay clear of drugs as they are an impediment to true progress.

The only way to achieve mental management is through practice. I see so many books in the shops on management and they sell extremely well. Managing business, management relations with the shop floor, quick management where everything can be accomplished within sixty seconds, manage your this, manage your that. Why can't I find a book on the shelves called *Manage your Mind*.

I wonder why this subject is overlooked by so many successful personal development authors. I see them writing about mental tricks ... the utilisation of certain knowledge to find out what the other person is thinking for selfish gain, yet I believe such selfish gain is the most sure fire method of losing any power that may come your way through use of these tricks. It has long been a well known fact that knowledge of the Ageless Wisdom utilised purely for selfish reasons is nothing less than black magic. Voodoo works by telling someone that they are a certain negative way and letting *them* turn such a suggestion into a *self fulfilling prophecy*.

Currently fashionable tricks of the business include watching the position of a person's eyes in response to your communication; this will tell you whether their primary mode of operation is visual, auditory or kinaesthetic; so you can use it to have your way with them? I have described such technology myself in earlier work, but discovered much to my dissatisfaction that it was usually studied for selfish reasons only. I therefore now avoid it, and concentrate on tools which are much more powerful and less easily abused, because assimilation of such data involves a comprehension of the privileges that go with this understanding, and the perils of abuse.

What I offer you is called *PAC Magic*. The methods used

come under the generic heading of *PAC Alchemy*, a modern form of the ancient art. TTM (Time To Myself) is PAC Magic at its simplest. It involves you with yourself and nobody else, not because of any leaning towards separateness; more for reasons to do with the old adage that *charity begins at home*, and another old saying which states that *you are never in better company than yourself!* Getting it right in your own universe is an important step towards the honourable goal of interdependence with other human beings.

I spoke about the subject of emptying ones head to a learned friend of mine, who responded with the fact that you cannot ever empty your head! A mind is constantly filled with information ... much as the lady at the PAC Gathering had stated! He continued to say that it was an ability to tune out from certain frequencies that I was describing as an attribute to aspire towards. This I agree with totally. We must remember that the mind is a transmitter and a receiver, and I often recall Napoleon Hill writing about *not forgetting to turn off the receiver*, which comprises part of your brain.

TTM is learning to control your personal radio set!

Of course the brain is not only used for the transmission and reception of mental energy. It is also your own personal biological computer. In fact it is the most sophisticated computer ever built anywhere, and you have one all to yourself. The latest Pentium technology does not even approach its power. It is completely upgradeable, but has one contra to all of its pros ... it does not come with a manual!

This you must compile from a working knowledge of it, much like some people do with pirate software for their computers. Because the data has been illegally copied onto floppy disc, there are no hard copy instructions accompanying it ... sometimes there are on board tutorials, but in the main it is a case of trial and error. This analogy is quite fair, but most unfortunate.

Perhaps written instructions are scant deliberately. Such scarcity stimulates and encourages a development of sensitivity to our own vibrations, and a trusting of our personal intuition.

Find an environment where stillness, solitude and quiet will not be offensive to anyone else, and preferably where there is nobody else. Instigate these qualities into your surroundings and sit comfortably in whichever position suits you. Close your eyes. You are about to get acquainted with your inner world. Latch onto a stray thought and explore it ... flow love to it ... change it ... let it slip away. Allow another thought to come into your field of perception and repeat this process quite a few times, until you begin to establish rapport within. Acknowledge the blackness or any other colour that may be visible. Applying my golden rule of *Gradual Graduation*, begin the process of domination over this mental property which is under your jurisdiction.

Your goal for this action is the ability to *just be there!* You must therefore stop the manifestation of any thought form as soon as you become aware of it. This is your world and not a play area for any old stray mental matter. You must be determined yet gradual. We seek long term results, and not transient gain which passes on immediately the next fad shows up. Now is the time to stamp your authority on your mental universe.

Your first TTM should last around two minutes. Increase this time period to four, five, six and seven minutes; until eventually you are able to be there for perhaps fifteen minutes. This is not a perseverance test, so only exercise as much as is comfortable for you. Once you have dominance over this world, you may desist from this activity, and reinstate it at will ... as and when it could prove beneficial. If you have reached the end phenomenon of TTM, and then find that one day you are suddenly mentally overwhelmed, find a retreat and regain dominance. You now know how to exert this authority.

When you have practiced and perfected your TTM technique, then I suggest you consider utilising it, without being obvious and irritating to others, wherever and whenever you need to ... *without* seeking the aid of a sympathetic environment. You may be at work ... following a disagreement with your superior; use TTM. On the Underground in London or the Subway in America ... the noise may be antagonistic to your peace of mind; use TTM. In the car with the Family ... a fellow motorist in Newcastle has interpreted the rules of giving way to traffic from the right already on the roundabout, differently to you ... the visitor to California does not know that you can turn right on a red light if the way is clear, and you are stuck behind him; use TTM.

I know that you will find this ability to empty your head at will, an indispensable attribute precious to your ascension up the PAC Ladder and onto better states. Practice and perfect it. The technique is at your service and will oblige you well.

Where do we go when asleep?
The same place we end up at after death of the physical body. Does this surprise you?

There are three aspects of human being relevant to this section of the book. There is the physical body, which is obvious to the naked eye. There is the astral body, sometimes known as the desire body, which is connected to emotions and exists on a lower mental plane, which some feel has an illusory status, of which more and more people are becoming aware. Then there is the mental body, which exists on a plane of the same name; this is your inner world. The astral plane has the apparency of sharing your inner world with the mental plane, but as a separate entity it is not based on any universal principle, as is the mental plane.

When the physical body lies resting, the real you is released from its confinement!

If indiscriminate dreams are part of your sleeping process, then you will be partaking of the illusory astral plane life. Existence on this level is random and haphazard to say the least. It is emotional, and full of imagery which has found life in such an environment, but such life was often irrationally instigated. The higher animal kingdom can be conscious of this world, as well as most human beings. Faster vibrating beingnesses also operate on this plane as a *Service of Light to Humanity*. This spiritual force manifests astrally, because so many people live their emotional lives within this world, and it would be less likely to encounter them elsewhere.

The modern alchemist is in the business of transmuting the unknown and unexplored, into the advantages and knowledge of tomorrow. For this reason it is important to be cognisant of all inner world phenomena, and if any scepticism is apparent on your part, then it must be asked of yourself if you are to be allowed the privilege of experiment in exploration. PAC Alchemy is a generic heading covering the utilisation and transmutation of any previously unknown inner and outer world laws, into practical aids and benefits for both yourself and fellow mankind.

It is a PAC axiom that states ... *improvement of personal life through positive attitudes, benefits humanity as a whole.*

It is for this reason that new and powerful techniques are being made available to you ... it is for individuals to ensure that any abilities uncovered within themselves and made available for their own gain, will always have at the very least, group benefit as a by product.

Remember the Great Law which states, *"to those who give all, all is given."*

The astral world is a constant reminder of all that is grabbing about people. It has the apparency of being glamourous and can suck you into its ploy of want and have and take and lust and cry and laugh and hate and judge! It is also a world which, to the degree that we concentrate on it, is available to us, and as such should be understood and utilised for any benefits which could be forthcoming.

⋏

If you would like to know more about this subject, then you can study the work of Djwhal Khul, written by Alice A Bailey, and published by the Lucis Press Ltd, Suite 45, 3, Whitehall Court, London SW1A 2EF. I suggest a compilation volume called *Ponder on This*. Write the information down, and get into action by ordering this book!

Patricia Diane Cota-Robles also speaks about these realms in an enlightening way on some of her excellent recordings. You may like to order a catalogue list which is available from The New Age Study of Humanity's Purpose, PO Box 41883, Tucson, Arizona 85717, USA.

If you have filled your body full of food which has not been digested before sleep, then part of your rejuvenating process will be squandered on this procedure. If your body has been saturated with alcohol, then the liver will work furiously to strain this drug from your system. These descriptions are of course the opposite of relaxation. If however, your regimen includes sensible diet and habit, of which more later in this book, then you will feel safe enough to utilise your sleep period as *soul time*.

This is TTM at its most spiritual. You can train yourself to

40

avoid the astral illusion by concentration and singleness of purpose, affirmed to and by yourself, before sleeping! If you achieve mental domination before sleeping, with the intention of soul enrichment during this rest period, then perhaps such guidance as would enhance the quality of the soul will be forthcoming. This is not to say that someone else is going to do the amelioration work to you. Advanced PAC Practitioners understand that a little guidance from One Who Knows, is worth more than a thousand blind alleys of research, which are themselves little harbingers of greater things to come.

It must be stated also that you can decide to plunge headlong into the astral world of emotion and glamour for kicks and meaningless pastime; it is not wrong of me to point this out to you, as it is a phenomenon which will become obvious as you begin delving into your own universe. It is not the purpose of this book however, which is a practical volume of guidance based on progress along the Evolutionary Path towards greater awareness and consciousness.

Mention may also be made here of a scientific approach to the subject of Lucid Dreaming made by Doctor Stephen LeBerge, in Stanford, California. He has spent over ten years researching this field in his *sleep laboratory*. He has developed electronic aids as well as mental disciplines to potentially increase the number of these lucid dreams one can have. Linked to this research are *computer-like* machines, called *Dream Lights*, which can be programmed and even interfaced with a computer. They have sensors inside a blindfold mask which recognize REM, or, *Rapid Eye Movement* sleep. This REM is a signal that one is dreaming. The sensors activate little lights in the mask which blink at a pre-set speed, and one sees these little lights as part of the dream. If all goes well, you are eventually conscious of the *Dream Lights*, which are indicating that you are dreaming what you are seeing. The first few times, you may awaken excitedly, but with practice, one begins to hold this state of awareness, having made the first crawl toward self awareness or self realisation. The word crawl is used, because there is such an infinity of development remaining ahead before one could be considered *walking*. The machine sells for around $1200, which is quite a lot of money, and certainly enough to deter all but the most resolute. I believe that there is a cheaper and less sophisticated version called the *NovaDreamer* for about $275.

There is also a book on the subject called *Exploring the World of Lucid Dreaming*. There are memberships available, a Newsletter, and they refer to each other as *Oneironauts*, which I think means *dream-flyer*, or *dream traveller*. More information is available from *The Lucidity Institute, 2555 Park Boulevard, Suite 2, Palo Alto, California 94306, USA.*

I prefer to concentrate on the natural phenomena at our disposal for the training of abilities in this area and include information about Lucid Dreaming as an aspect of the subject which some people seem to find beneficial.

Sleep can be utilised as a tool for the enhancement of your everyday life. It is a unique opportunity to almost automatically glimpse a state which most people around the planet fear, which is that of death. *The more we die ... the more we live ...* is an ancient saying which I know to be true. If sleep is a version of this state which can be experienced whilst in possession of corporeal body, then surely that is an advantage which must be exploited for human gain. We must cultivate an ability to bring back into our human consciousness, whatever we are able to soul perceive on the mental plane whilst we are asleep.

Where do we go when asleep? ... *A little closer to home,* **is my answer.**

Write down experiences that you have been aware of during past sleep periods. Dreams, feelings, nightmares, desires, fears ... anything whatsoever, no matter how silly it may seem.

Illuminate a desire to sleep peacefully, by deliberately deciding to avoid meaningless adventure on the astral plane whilst asleep.

Before you close your eyes tonight, practice TTM ... empty your head and affirm a desire to get to know your true spiritual self whilst asleep.

Identity, or, ID Adoption

And so we progress ... onward and upward ever ... getting to know you and accepting yourself, whilst affirming a definite desire and commitment to improve, all the while understanding just what a vital process it is that you are involved with.

It is possible that people have entered your life at various times, to whom you have afforded positions of altitude, evident in your mental outlook upon them. It is a common human deficiency to confuse respect, with emotional attachment. It could be that you have regarded someone in high esteem, to the degree that you have taken on their identity so to speak, erroneously considering such adoption part of a winning formula. You are already a composite being, and this state is known as duality; the spirit combined with a physical vehicle. To employ the mannerism and beingness of another will weaken your powers even further.

This adoption of alternative identities is absolutely common amongst all strata of society. *The grass seems so much greener on*

43

the other side ... but of course it isn't! This phenomenon is a symptom of grossly undervaluing oneself. It is easier to see the positive attributes of another, than it is to look both within and without to glimpse ones own. Or is it? I think not and it is easily within your power to eliminate such identity adoption if indeed this is a trap into which you have been lured. The more you become accustomed and acclimatised to your private inner world, the easier it will be for you to correct any behaviour deficiencies that may come to light.

Such Identity, or ID, substitutions are also common amongst those who belong to certain fanatical groups, or are affiliated in some aberrant way to particularly extremist teachings. These people can seem to take an age before answering a simple question, because they have to compute the answer through their perception of the so called winning viewpoint, which they have unwittingly made their mentor.

Stay true to yourself and honour your own judgement. I guarantee that for you, there is no one better qualified than you, to be you. When someone is talking to you, or asking your opinion about specific things, it is you they wish to address, and not some invisible viewpoint which manifests uncomfortably and weakly through your interpretation of it.

Each time you discover something negative about yourself, it will enable you to get self acquainted just a little bit more. With each balancing of this revealed negativity, comes a deeper and more beneficial knowledge of the real you. Don't ever be afraid to self confess your shortcomings ... it is such disclosure which will transform every single admission into an ingredient for success.

Advanced PAC Practitioners talk to themselves and accept only the truth!

Sometimes this ID Adoption has reached a stage where it has become subliminal ... a person does not know that it is occurring. How does such a victim delete this type of file from the internal computer? It is only by watching and listening to yourself, and your observations of how you interact with others, that will give you this valuable data.

If you catch yourself ID Adopting then stop it! *Exert Will* and stop it! Examine any recurring patterns such as ... every time you are asked if you like classical music: you remember the other ID mentioning a love of Beethoven Concertos; you find yourself wondering if the other ID likes all classical music ... you risk assuming the reply to your enquiry would be affirmative and answer yes ... long after any interest to that response has diminished. This process takes an abnormal amount of time and can be infuriating to a non understanding colleague.

✎

Make a list of all the people whom you admire. Prepare another inventory of anyone whom you feel to be overpowering towards you. Thirdly, write down the names of any person known, who has defeated you in any way shape or form.

✪

Shine a light on your reaction to these lists. Ponder the word *Identity*.

🏃

Assert the right to your own identity by demonstrating a recovered viewpoint of your own, previously masked by this curiosity of ID Adoption.

As you can see from this guide, there is more to knowledge of oneself that may be immediately evident. To proceed on a course of personal development would be wasteful if you indulged in it utilising someone elses point of view. The adopted ID within its rightful owner would not benefit either ... this makes such behaviour a complete waste of time. I therefore recommend that you treat this subject with active and enthusiastic endeavour, so that as much of the real *you* will manifest and benefit from what is now to follow.

I now invite you to explore *the feelings from within* ...

the feelings from within

Guide Two

the feelings from within

When to a man who understands, the self has become all things ... *Vagasaneyi, Samhita, Upanishad. Translated by F Max Mueller, in Volume 1 of 146, page 312*

Cultivating Intuition

... immediate perception by the mind without reasoning ... is one of the definitions given by the Cassell paperback English Dictionary of this often misused word from our language. I begin Guide Two with this explanation, not because I entirely endorse the message transmitted by it; more to draw attention to the fact that our regular lexicons are both an essential tool for personal development, and, that such aids can blow you off course if you do not *feel* beyond what you have read. It is also this word *feel* that can lead to misunderstanding of the *Intuition Concept*, and consequent denial of any successful cultivation thus far achieved.

We have bound the meaning of intuition tightly within a heavy shroud of materialistic comprehension. We must distinguish sharply between an understanding of the mind, and a reaching out towards *soul consciousness*.

Gut feelings have little or nothing to connect them intrinsically with intuition, except perhaps that they could be deemed the physical harmonic of this faculty that I am about to describe. Gut feeling is related to instinctive anxiety, both methods being also utilised as survival routine in the animal kingdom. The corporeal reality of *knowing*, is a useful tool, but you must accept that it is based around computations used by the majority of people, rather than cosmic phenomena, which we are now adding to the list of magical ingredients for our assault on success.

When you collect knowledge by means of the intellect, it is

49

stored by the mind and accessed by you through utilisation of the physical brain. This is useful, and has been a survival and personal enhancement technique employed for many thousands of years by the human race ... it will continue and thrive as a modus operandi. Indeed, we will hone the cutting edge of this method as time goes by, transforming it beyond present comprehension into a thoroughly streamlined and user friendly instrument.

Humanity has an insatiable desire to assimilate knowledge. The intellect has been elevated in status towards a pinnacle of aspiration for much of Occidental mankind. Omniscience is an honourable incarnate intent, yet lethally dangerous without an accompanying development of the heart. This type of correlation between the head and the heart is also alien to much western thought.

SK

Mention might be made here regarding the present scientific community's knowledge about the left brain, which deals with fact and intellect, and the right brain which handles artistry and intuition. Also of interest may be the occult knowledge that intellect is the energy associated with the Throat Chakra (Will, Power, and the Father-God in the Holy Trinity, color ... Sapphire Blue), and that intuition is the energy associated with the Heart Chakra (Love, Compassion, Forgiveness, and the Mother-God...Holy Spirit...in the Holy Trinity, color ... Crystalline Pink). We of course, are the Son/Daughter (Color Violet) in the Holy Trinity when the Father-God (Sapphire Blue) and the Mother-God (Crystalline Pink) are in perfected balance. That's what all this is about, isn't it Phil?
... end of note.

PAC Alchemy demands the utilisation of any beneficial ingredients in a quest for true success; Advanced PAC Practitioners always surmount the barrier of previously held sacrosanct beliefs in the light of fresh evidence.

We tend to utilise the heart poetically, to describe love and affection, but what would happen if we considered it for one moment, as an actual organ of love ... unconditional love ... Divine Love...unemotional love ... etheric love ... cosmic love ... love born of ever increasing and total perception!

Just as you have a mental and astral body, so too do you own a physical body ... *which is an exact replica of your etheric body*. This etheric body is related to the substance known as ether ... it is solid and physical, yet, because it is comprised of ether, the etheric body is invisible to most of us. As we evolve, so too will we become more conscious of etheric bodies, and this new awareness will apparently happen sooner rather than later. This etheric form is functional as a medium for and transmitter of, cosmic energy necessary for your corporeal performance on this physical plane, whether you are cognisant of the phenomenon or not. It is also the place where some believe all individual past experience to be recorded. The etheric body transmits energy to seven major centres, called Chakras, or Power Centers, and twenty nine lesser centres within the physical frame. These centres are worthy of further separate study beyond the scope of this book, and I once again suggest the work of *Djwhal Khul written by Alice Bailey*, for the sensible approach to this subject, which is fast becoming the modern equivalent to Parlour Psychology of the 60s, 70s and 80s.

The phrase *Kundalini Fire* flows off the tongue with ease, yet it describes the very energy of the universe itself. Such potent force and any premature attraction of it should be avoided, if contact is artificially manipulated. This universal energy becomes available naturally to a person whose endeavours firstly require it, and secondly ... much more importantly ... whose service of others in an attitude of humility illustrates a trueness of living in the light of the soul. I mention and stress this point now, as the theory of centres, or chakras, that I have mentioned, and Kundalini Fire, are often incorporated into many new age healing techniques. This theory, when practiced, is fine in the hands of experts, but I have no way of conveying how to avoid the charlatans, *except by encouraging you to cultivate your own intuition.*

The heart is one of the centres that I have mentioned; the life, energy and power of this centre is felt within an individual life to the extent that it has been cultivated and allowed to flow into and be a part of the very beingness of the self. As the intellect grows, so too should the love power of the heart, as it is this organ which will conceptually channel the knowledge from the mind, along a course of action in keeping with acceptable methods for the achievement of success.

The intellect is a cold world and needs the warming qualification of the heart. Knowledge accumulated in the mind is often used to contrive gut reactions, and these responses are formulated through a processing of cold data, however worthless this processing may have been. The heart aids the process by approaching situations in a more humanistic fashion.

Real intuition is a soul quality!

A *Mystical* approach to life will afford a person a way forward through feelings only. An *Occult* approach involves the pure fact of enquiry into hidden or veiled truth. The *Esotericists* blend these two avenues together for what I consider to be a pragmatic and holistic approach to contemporary living. It involves the bringing together of the head and the heart; it is a safe and non fanatical way to uncover previously concealed knowledge and universal laws, with a view to practical application in the modern world.

The word *esoteric*, literally means, *intended for or understood by only a small group ... not publicly disclosed.* We are in the business of making exoteric much of what was previously undisclosable, with the proviso that utilisation of these revelations will be for honourable gain only. This involves you in some mind twisting wrestles within, but any effort will be amply rewarded.

Intuition is a phenomena which presently can only be experienced in a weaker harmonic form of its full pristine glory; however, the power of this harmonic is far greater than the gut feelings which I have mentioned earlier. The way to foster intuition is via TTM, onward into meditation.

Intuition and Meditation

Many volumes have been written on the subject of meditation, and this work acknowledges such effort. I am merely going to take from the theory and practice of meditation what is required for the purposes of this book, and trust that your studies will continue with the subject in greater detail for your own benefit.

Words act like triggers. They fire off preconceived assumptions and can often stop you in your tracks from progressing, if they are not to your liking. Meditation is a word that can bring forth pictures in your mind of monks dressed in orange robes, chanting, and bearing about as much resemblance to what you want from life as does a child's drawing of a bonfire night rocket to the space shuttle. The Hare Krsna Movement is often mentioned as a barrier to the acceptance of much eastern philosophy; probably because they shave their heads and happily dance along streets clinking cymbals. Buddhist Evenings for groovy groups of young hopefuls can often dash the future of any aspiring inner world explorer who gets caught up with his contemporaries who are merely looking for an impossible quick fix from the spiritual world. The Beatles reportedly flirted with eastern religion through a mentor called the Maharishi Mahesh Yogi ... I know that their apparent disillusionment caused many people to stay clear of *what they weren't used to*, **without ever trying it!** This is your challenge if you are affected in this way by words ... and I know that many readers will be.

I have no grumble with any of these groups or people whom I mention; I write about them only in an effort to make you *re-look* if you have *shut-off;* and if you are new to this sphere of thought, then it is as well that I warn you anyway of examples that may deter your enjoyment and full involvement in *everything* the world has to offer you.

TTM has given you some control over your mind, but it has not steered your thoughts in any particular direction. Meditation when connected to the fostering of a contact with the Intuitive Self, and at most other times, is an essential medium.

⊜𝕂

If we have arrived at the point of understanding what or who we *really* are ... a Being which *has* a body, a mind and a name; and for lack of a better title we use *The I AM* to describe this Being, then we must understand that this being is an absolute marvel of versatility. We can watch and listen to a *One Man Band* playing several different instruments with his feet, hands, elbows, knees, even his head, shoulders, and who knows what else, all at the same time. This is a very low and weak example of what *The I AM* is capable of doing. *The I AM* can hold its attention on a myriad of things, activities and places, all at the same time. If there was a way of measuring how much of its attention was expended in each direction emanating from a 360 degree sphere, we might be able to see or calculate how much of it is devoted to these various targets. For analogy only we can say it has a purely arbitrary total of 500,000 Attention Units. At a given moment it could have 200 AUs on driving its car, 500 AUs on listening to the soccer game on the radio, 10 AU on the bad weather, 50 AUs on a pretty girl in view, not to mention things like overdue bills and the angry boss. Note that some of these AUs are on automatic in the subconscious portion of the mind ... like driving the car ... but *The I AM* is definitely aware of directing many other AUs; like the pretty girl crossing the street! I am sure you get the idea without me prolonging the explanation. The point is that *The I AM* literally places itself where its ATTENTION is. This attention, as we

54

touched on above, is sometimes self-directed by an act of WILL, which could start as curiosity, interest or desire. It could be initiated by some sudden impingement *grabbing* your attention, like a threat, or opportunity ... a child runs into the street, or the pretty girl from the previous analogy smiles invitingly! I go into this in such detail to arrive at greater understanding, and acceptance I hope, of the maxim ...

You Are Where Your ATTENTION *Is!*

... and I hope that we have now advanced enough to understand we are not referring to where your *body* is. Surely we have all used the expression *not here* in reference to someone not apparently conscious of present time, or even to ourselves in similar circumstances. There is great wisdom to be found in some colloquialisms. Now comes the reason why I am stressing this under the heading of Intuition and *Meditation*. Meditation is a self-directed action. If we are where our ATTENTION is, where are we most of the time? Life *demands* our attention ... making a living, raising the family, television, the news, taking care of the body, the wife or husband ... where are ALL these things that *demand* our attention, which is where we *are*? They are in this physical plane of *Personalities*, referred to as such in the writings of Alice Bailey, who describes it perfectly, with all its problems and sufferings, in spite of some beauty and joy. What we are attempting to do I think, is get people to raise their awareness into a higher level by focussing the ATTENTION on higher planes ... where the *REAL Self* ... *The I AM* mainly dwells. I say mainly, because that is where most of those unused Attention Units are. Remember that we only really use about 10% of our brains potential! I expect for most of us it is even less when translated into Attention Units. So, unless we are born Ascended Masters or Saints, few of us will ever be aware of *The I AM*, or these higher planes of *Light*, unless we make the effort of exercising simple TTM, and then advance to rhythmical, (same time every day) practise of *guided* meditation. You have already touched on the importance of opening your awareness to the *right* influences. Mediums, now often called Channels, Tarot, Fortune Telling, Ouija

55

Boards and Crystal Gazing may be fun and interesting, but such activity is not going to get us acquainted with *The I AM*, except by us getting bored with them and deciding that they are just titillating and interesting, but unfulfilling steps along The Real Path. The POWER we are talking about? THAT is the SOURCE! I wish it could be put in 50 feet letters on a 1000 feet high billboard ...

> **NONE WILL REACH THE HIGHER DOMAINS UNLESS A CONTINUED EFFORT IS MADE TO *PROPERLY* MEDITATE. THE MATERIAL PLANE EXERTS A CONSTANT PULL BACK DOWN ON THE ASPIRANT.**
> *... end of note.*

Make a list of three times that gut feelings have led you into particular courses of action. If the results have been positive then congratulate your lower instincts ... if they have not, then still positively acknowledge the existence of these impulsive sensations.

Illuminate two concepts with fresh thought and enthusiasm. They are ... *body* ... then ... *soul*.

Sit quietly and comfortably, in a space where you will not be disturbed. Practice TTM until you are *at cause* over your mental universe. When you have achieved this dominance, introduce a *thought for germination*. This reflection will be inspired by the phrase *I Am The Source Point*.

You are the *Source Point of You,* and it is this aspect of your beingness which will afford you the privilege of access onto the Intuitional Plane. It is a passage of *Gradual*

Graduation ... big trees *will* grow from little acorns ... you are instigating a process with which you must pledge to remain, until your goal of daily intuitive contact has been fulfilled. This fulfillment will be practically illustrated by a reflection of this new mental capacity into your physical existence. The aim of this meditation is to *touch your soul* and *access intuition*. Practice this journey into your inner world whenever you can, and you will discover that you penetrate deeper and further into the darkness with each mission undertaken.

You may get *hooked* to the point of using meditation as an escape from the reality and responsibilities placed upon you by your material existence. You can, by persisting in this practice, get such exquisite experience and enlightenment that you may feel a desire to abandon the material world entirely. As with many aspects of living, the goal is *balance*. We do not stay in bed forever because it is so restful and refreshing, and nor should we become fanatical about meditation. However, I think we can agree that for most of us we are a very long way from *balance*, and consequently even further from *over balance*. This note should be a caution to you, and an illustration of possibilities we should all be aware of.

You will have noted by this point in the book that few of the practical routines outlined herein, have definite end points which can be instantly demonstrated in your life as successfully assimilated attributes. They are all part of the *Gradual Graduation* process *which lasts* ...

Walking on coals as representative of your domination over the lower self is catchy, gimmicky and incredibly attractive to many ... it has its place in the world of personal development ... much as have many psyche-up techniques, like constant affirmation of the words Yeah! Yeah! Yeah! Or, *every day I am getting better and better ... and ... BETTER!!!* ...which is the Sylva Mind Control way of starting a session. Punching through a sheet of hardboard can be fun, and physically representative of breaking through your own mental barriers. By all means restate these symbolic gestures as often as you wish, and if they bring with them a deeper and long lasting enjoyment of life for you, then they are justified as legitimate exercises within your own modus operandi and should be accorded such status as they deserve.

You must understand that these exercises are personality type tricks and bear little relation to what I am teaching. They are however, a constant obstacle to personal development teachers like myself, as they have the *lime light* shone on them, whilst I am extolling virtues of the *soul light*. Lime light is instant and glamourous, but soon passes on to the next object of transient interest ... soul light is more gradual in its intensity, but *eternal!*

Glamour is a tricky subject to deal with ... if I condemn it, I risk losing any audience I may have attracted, *before the lesson has begun!* I do not condemn or condone it; in true non committal and unbiased style ... I acknowledge it.

Acceptance of the Universe is an indication of our self developmental stage. Stating, *I accept all that is*, with understanding, verbally indicates your own inner judgement of yourself, and the degree of true achievement thus far accomplished in your particular process. *Every single thing, act, and condition is exactly the way it is supposed to be, given the causes that are at work!* Using this data as an excuse for indolence, over activity, money grabbing, sloppiness or one pointed determination to the detriment of many, is also an indication of your true level of under achievement! Glamour and personality type attitudes must be accepted with understanding.

The PAC has a policy of interdependence with other like minded groups. Sometimes I get calls asking how many members we have ... I no longer relay this information as it is irrelevant ... an instant comparison is numerically made with other membership lists and a qualitative assessment made on that basis. If I wanted the PAC judged by its number of members then I would go out and recruit more. Instead, I concentrate on *quality* and people just come along through my books, and word of mouth ... some join ... most stay!

The PAC is not how big it is! The Visualisation Statement relates a desire for a constantly growing membership ... this is exactly what we have ... with no broken promises. The only *honorable* justification for wanting or having a huge, worldwide PAC, is that Humanity and this Planet would *divinely* benefit from it ... and perhaps the PAC could become a big factor in establishing the aspiration *On Earth As It Is In Heaven*. I know this is a challenging statement to make, and has been used by every type of money-making, power-mad, mind-controlling group from Charles Manson to Communism, other-isms to even some of our highly revered religious organisations. I would hope that possible challengers to the statement would hold back any attack until they fully understand to the point of acceptance, the powerful effect THOUGHT FORMS are having on our existence right now, *at this very moment!* All the police, armies, prisons, laws, and whatever else can be physically contrived, will not make one iota of change to the mess this world currently finds itself in, until Humanity, the only force that can creatively think, emanates the right THOUGHT FORMS through meditation and deliberate concentration, in line with creating a HEAVEN right here on EARTH.

We've got the whole world resting in our hands!

It is in our hands *alone!* You must understand that it is only Humanity who are able to perform this cure! That means BIG group action! ... lots of *MINDS* thinking the *right* THOUGHT FORMS. To say that the PAC is the only group dedicated to this goal would be a huge lie. The New Group of World Servers, the Light Workers, some Theosophically oriented groups, The Rosicrucian Fellowship and grouped people of goodwill everywhere, are also dedicated, to the degree that they are in action on this subject. There are many thousands of people already engaged in this caring activity, and many billions yet to comprehend the power and responsibility connected with personal thought!

Attention lodged firmly in the World of Personalities causes people to care who owns the biggest group, and who has the most prestige or recognition. *It is more fulfilling to keep your attention on the game instead of the score.* If any challengers see the whole picture of the PAC, the big picture, they may we hope, conclude that we are not just repeating worn out claims by stating our goals and potentialities; nor are we original with the information we make available. Throughout the ages, there have been teachers of wisdom helping us humans to establish Heaven on Earth. Their methods began with esoteric teachings, which, probably with good intent, were adopted by enthusiastic groups into exoteric religions. But, in this plane of personalities, divisions and strife were bound to arise, until, in our present age, a huge majority now disillusioned and confused, are placing their faith more into newer approaches which rely less on someone else ... a wrathful God, a Priest or a Preacher. Guilt feelings for example, are no longer relevant if they ever were, for the achievement of peace and freedom from past misdemeanors. Most people are willing to listen to a scientific approach, and the PAC attempts to render the Teachings in just that manner, and to the best of its ability. *As a man thinketh in his heart, so is he!* If we apply scientific pondering to such ancient aphorisms, they usually make tremendous sense.

The PAC is a reflection of this book. We believe in success and actively seek to partake of this physical world to its fullest possibilities. We also believe in possessions ... as long as you understand that you are not them ... *you are not what you have!*

To conclude this guide to intuition ... I need *not* mention the power that the attribute of intuition will give you.

Logic versus Inner Knowing

If intuition exists on a plane of its own, affording any visitor to the intuitional level a glimpse or study of the sum total of everything ever thought by mankind, then inner knowing is the individual soul quality which each of us is able to utilise within ourselves, and perhaps a more pragmatic concept to embrace. Inner knowing calls on the heart for direction and uses the intellect for fact.

Various Sherlock Holmes movies have illustrated the *logical hero* as a walking deductive computer. The very latest of these films based around this character that I have seen is the 1993 movie called *1994 Baker Street: Sherlock Holmes Returns*. In this film, the great detective comes back to modern day life and engages a descendent of his evil arch enemy Moriarty. His intellect and *power* of deduction is still grippingly sharp, but of course his conclusions are invariably wrong as they are formed from intelligence assembled around 90 years earlier. Reference to a sixties *hippy*, inspired mental pictures of a large posterior to him. The New York vernacular word *cool*, became *cold*, when he needed to exaggerate its meaning.

This treatment of Sherlock was a good illustration for our purposes, of the shortcomings connected with the intellect when it is used without qualification. The logical intellect is an analytical computer which has little leaning towards sentiment or feelings.

The heart is more inclined towards that feeling described as occurring just beneath it in the solar plexus area ... gut feeling ... with the added advantage of love, coupled with its innate power as a centre intrinsically connected to the etheric body.

I like to describe inner knowing, as the harmonic of intuition presently available to us. It is an imperfect tool which relies on an amount of feeling, influenced somewhat by past experiences, mixed with some intellectual ingredients and blended with an amount of animal instinct. It is not what I suggest you aim for as the goal of your meditation which formed the preceding practical exercise ... it *is* a practical tool which is immediately accessible, and even more powerful now that you now how to differentiate between the various harmonics of this subject matter.

There should not be any antagonism between logic and inner knowing. Both endowments should be called upon in tandem, and independently respected as interdependent qualities.

○

After establishing the meaning of the words *poetry* and *fact* ... ponder their meanings and note your feelings in connection with them.

✎

Look at an animal and briefly list its skills in a factual way. Describe its features accurately. On another page set your feelings free and compose a poem about this animal. Use analogy and metaphor, but do not worry too much about style and content.

I wandered lonely as a cloud, is an example of a famous opening line composed by one of our best known poets. From the inspiring novel Wuthering Heights, written by Emily Brontë, is another stunning example of a heartfelt use of words ... *She was the most winning thing that ever brought sunshine into a desolate house. A real beauty in face, with the Earnshaw's handsome dark eyes but the Linton's fair skin and small features, and yellow curling hair. Her spirit was high, though not rough, and qualified by a heart sensitive and lively to excess in its affections. That*

capacity for intense attachments reminded me of her mother; still,
she did not resemble her, for she could be soft and mild as a dove,
and she had a gentle voice and pensive expression. Her anger was
never furious, her love never fierce. It was deep and tender.

This description is one of the most effective combinations of
poetry and fact ... spirit and body ... that I have ever come
across.   It is remarkable in that it conjures up an exactness
of mental picture, without ever sacrificing beautiful prose to
the demands of accurate explanation. I hope these two examples
help if you are not used to writing poetry. Do not however, judge
yourself against them as that would be irrelevant to our intent.

↳

When the next two opportunities arise in your life where
there is nothing particularly important at stake ... *in a*
situation where ordinarily you would have utilised logic,
substitute a poetic approach ... then vice versa ... *substitute*
logic when your approach would have been lyrical.

You have to practice these exercises to benefit from them!

Advanced PAC Practitioners are cognisant of the duality within
them. Spirit and body together produces many blends of a similar
nature in everyday life. This information is offered for practical
application into everyday existence; if you find yourself drifting
away from an attachment to the sentiments in this book, then revise
the pages you have already covered and discover if you may have
passed a word or concept that you did not fully understand.

Are the end phenomena of the ✎ ✪ ⚡ 𝄞 occurring for you?
These exercises are designed for you to self-cognite ... are you
cogniting? If not then you must re-apply yourself to each section
that has not *hit home* for you.

The Flows that You Transmit

As your abilities increase, so does your circle of influence. Your power will grow in an exact ratio to your practical exhibition of responsibility in everyday activities. Lip service is no deceiver of physical law. Many people are responsible for the bringing about in others, of certain undesirable sensations and emotions. Often, mental feelings about a colleague are in direct contradiction to the physical demonstrations and social intercourse that exists between two people. Sometimes a negative thought slips out into a demonstrative action ... a question may follow by the recipient of this unscheduled outburst ... *is that the way you really feel about me? ... is something bugging you? ... are you upset with me? ... have we a misunderstanding about my intentions here?* ... can all be examples of someone sensing that all is not as has been stated within a relationship. When replies ensue such as ... *of course not ... whatever gave you that idea? ... I would tell you if there was a problem ... I'm sure I duplicate your aims and I know they are honourable* ... and the opportunity to confront any contentious issue is not taken, damage follows and there is *no* excuse.

Your denial of a colleague's sensing of upset is criminal, as it throws doubt on any development of intuition, whether animal or spiritual, he or she may have fostered over the years. You must own up if guilty, and accept the consequences ... they will always be heralders of better times ahead.

You are constantly flowing the contents of your mind into the universe; as your abilities increase in value, so must your control of personal flows. It is now a well accepted fact that thoughts are the precursors of their physical counterparts. Feelings are equally transmittable, and as a department of the emotional wave length, they are dealt with astrally. As the majority of people are not yet *openly* conversant with the astral plane, and consequently unable to manage their affairs on this wave length as well as they already do on the physical plane, it is cruel to act duplicitously on this level.

You must make a commitment to honesty of communication ... this is a high ideal and an easy one to betray. You will be a better person for displaying restraint in any sphere of life that could prove damaging to your fellow man, and I urge you to polish your communication skills until they shine and distinguish you from the clutter of less radiant intercourse.

The basic skill that we should all aim for is purity of thought. Suppressing critical contemplations is an excellent way to launch a crusade in search of this high ideal. Your mental flows are a less dense form of matter than is conversation. Great conversationalists are those who have honed and cultivated an ability to *listen with interest*. Any oral contact utilised by such people is invariably non critical, an effort to stimulate further communication of a higher standard from the recipient, and *the verbal equivalent of a smile*. If your mental flows can approximate these conversational ideals which were admirably taught by Dale Carnegie, and can be studied in his book written in the thirties called *How To Win Friends and Influence People*, then you will progress in your quest for success at a very rapid rate.

✎

Make a list of seven critical habits that have crept into your modus operandi whilst you were not paying attention. Examples could be ... *indicating the contra side, after someone has excitedly related a story of good fortune which has just come their way ... goading a child after an achievement, by mentioning that you still think they can do better ... shouting at other drivers when you think that their handling of a traffic situation is not what you think it should be.* There are many examples I could give, as you can well imagine!

✪

Allow more light into the world by committing yourself to

the eradication of all critical tendencies. Think positively about yourself as a wise and intuitive attribute to humanity.

Utilising as few words as possible, the very next time you are in a situation which ordinarily would have stimulated you to verbal criticism ... flow *unconditional love and understanding* instead.

During my research for this book I discovered a man who always *thought* the words *God Bless You* whenever he had to resolve problems with angry customers ... and *it worked miracles for him.*

Unconditional Love

As I have already mentioned this concept in the previous action exercise, it is as well that the subject was scheduled for treatment so soon afterwards. There are few things more perturbing than constantly grazing yourself against unfamiliar expressions whilst reading a book. If this concept is unfamiliar, then I may be able to enlighten you.

Unconditional love is a flow *and* a state of being. Its presence is marked by a lack of critical outlook in both the communications and the actions of the person enjoying this concept of life. Criticism is one of the all time great traps that we have created for ourselves. When you criticise another, that very negative thought, word or deed, harnesses you to it and everything that it represents. Criticism is a ridge ... a rough edge ... disharmony! I mention it as an opposite, because of the ease of comparison you will discover when contrasting its intrinsic, negative inferiority, to the positive attributes of unconditional love, and degrees of this idealistic concept able to be experienced by the vast majority of mankind.

What are the practicalities of application to be viewed when approaching the subject of unconditional love? Vast are the benefits to yourself and others when such altruism is embraced;

this flippant phrase may sum up the very essence of all cosmic aspiration that we are able to contemplate.

Love is the quality that holds every aspect of existence together.

Part of my modus operandi in the field of personal development, is to take a high paragon in the purest possible form, and find its practical applications in our denser everyday life. This method frequently aligns the unseen with our corporeal capabilities, which I trust is not too irritating to those of us more used to concrete definitions. It is the direction and aspiration that is relevant ... this technique allows us to aim high! Remember that a mariner may use the North Star to guide him to his destination, without any desire to reach the galactic entity itself!

There are a number of evolved beings who assume massive amounts of earthly responsibility. To the best of my knowledge and research, they are Masters who have taken the fifth initiation and achieved a state which approximates being at full cause over physical life; these exalted members of the planet's races are also in possession of the advanced soul qualities such power would require as a prerequisite. Masters work day in day out, and night after night, on the physical, astral, mental and soul levels. They are sometimes still utilising the body of which they were in possession when taking their fifth initiation if they are in physical existence on the planet; although some Masters who are active within our sphere of awareness, according to karmic law, cannot descend lower than a particular plane. This was apparent around two thousand years ago, when the Master Jesus was baptised and agreed to become the vehicle for a Being who was not karmically able to descend beneath the astral plane. The Being known as The Christ thus utilised the physical sheath which the Master Jesus unselfishly made available to Him for His work.

The Christ boosted awareness on and around our planet, propelling evolution along its planned course with a principle known as *love-wisdom*. He also introduced the idea of forgiveness; a new and important aspect to progress for that particular time period. What He gave then in the form of a boost, was appropriate for that time period; this new Aquarian Age however, will also offer a stimulus to progress along the Path of a different yet similarly powerful nature, and stirrings are already being felt by many, as higher spiritual energies touch the lives of more and more people. The simple concepts of Love and Forgiveness are however, as relevant today as they ever have been; as demonstrated by both the Silent Knight Philosophy in its anonymous fashion, and physically by everyone to each other.

These Masters and Highly Evolved Beings that I write about, quite naturally *live* existence *as* Unconditional Love! Simple analogies will attest to their sacrifice ... can you imagine receiving your University Degree in Chemistry, only to spend the rest of your life striking matches; or, training to the standard of Chess Master and only ever playing the game with young children ... perhaps these analogies are inadequate, yet how else can such sentiments be transmitted. These Beings have evolved beyond the pull of karmic incarnation, yet stay with us to help!

Prove it, I hear you think; *perhaps*, is my reply!

Maybe an analogical quote from the HP Blavatsky book, *Isis Unveiled,* will illuminate your ponderings on this subject of belief in the unseen ...

Man-spirit proves God-spirit, as the one drop of water proves a source from which it must have come. Tell one who had never seen water, that there is an ocean of water, and he must accept it on faith or reject it altogether. But let one drop of it fall upon his hand, and he then has the fact from which all the rest may be inferred. After that he could by degrees understand that a boundless and fathomless ocean of water existed. Blind faith would no longer be necessary; he would have supplanted it with KNOWLEDGE. When one sees mortal man displaying tremendous capabilities, controlling the forces of nature and opening up to view the world of spirit, the reflective mind is overwhelmed with the conviction that if one man's spiritual *Ego* can do this much, the capabilities of the FATHER SPIRIT must be relatively as much vaster as the whole ocean surpasses the single drop in volume and potency. *Ex nihilo nihil fit;* prove the soul of man by its wondrous powers - you have proved God!

If unconditional love had not been constantly flowed onto our planet by stronger spiritual entities than are mainly incarnate on Earth at this present time, and have been throughout ancient history, evolution would be so retarded as to be almost useless from an experience point of view. So, this concept we call unconditional love exists and is practiced by *those who are able to be known.* I have already mentioned a Master earlier in this book, called Djwhal Khul, whose teaching work includes making esoteric knowledge more exoteric through many twentieth century books written by Alice A Bailey. This Master was also known in the nineteenth century to have shown H P Blavatsky many relevant pictures, and made her aware of substantial data, as well as dictating much of that classic and extensive work for which she accepted responsibility, known as *The Secret Doctrine*. DK as he is known, works closely with another Master called Koot Hoomi; this name is usually shortened to KH. The Master Morya is also frequently referred to in many works connected to the esoteric science. The Master Jupiter is the oldest of the Masters working in physical bodies for the sake of Humanity and is responsible for India, and the Master Rakoczi is another who is the Regent for Europe.

These Beings work with unconditional love and all its splendour; in order to do this they have transcended the need to operate with a personality, which is what most of us utilise as our visible representation of the soul, or *the real you*. The personality is that aspect of the soul closely connected to the body and operating with the apparency of a soul in physical incarnation. It is actually more closely related to the animal demeanor of man, and this fact is visible in the lack of long term values personality type people tend to attribute to much of their existence. This personality association is no longer either necessary, or attractive at this stage of our development, as we are now able to touch more significant aspects of the indwelling spirit. The character, which comprises more intrinsic spiritual qualities, is now available as an operating system, and it is up to the individual to contact character qualities as opposed to outmoded personality traits.

As your ability to transcend the personality increases, so will your capacity for unconditional love flourish. We have embraced this topic in our monthly Gatherings of the PAC, and the honest confession by some, of incapacity to touch this ideal, has been revealing.

What sets these PAC Practitioners apart from others is that they know about the concept and actively aspire towards it.

This is the Path!

The Path which is so often referred to in Theosophical, Rosicrucian, Esoteric, Mystical and Occult writings is so far removed from the mysterious, as to be openly amusing! The Path is *you* ... right here and now ... every time you improve some aspect of your life ... each time a new concept is embraced ... whenever you give ... with every cognition ... as you evolve ... through each act of love.

At the end of the Path is the Friendliest Force which is LO♡E. We must do our utmost to approximate whenever we can, the ideals of this Ultimate. Just as many young boys watch their favourite soccer players and emulate their skill; we can look at those who have won the right of living unconditional love, and begin to introduce the many ingredients into our lives of this universal wonder available to us all.

Forgiveness

One of the earliest enlightenments to come my way was a lesson in the power of forgiveness. As a word, it drifts in and out of fashion, yet it is universally known as a concept, encouraged and explained by some of the most loving and powerfully prophetic beings to ever grace our planet, yet rarely understood by many.

The potency of this act when reflected into your life, is quite unique and very closely related to unconditional love. The precursor to forgiveness is often a burning and degrading thought form or feeling inside, that has within it a certain amount of hate ... *the destroyer of the universe!* Hatred, dislike, resentment, loathing and abhorrence are all mental feelings which can cause physical illness. When higher spiritual energies are invoked into the vicinity of such negativity, they crystalise or solidify into low vibration matter, and such occurrence can be likened to the hardening of arteries in the human body, when dietary requirements have been abused.

Hatred is a sickness which surprisingly can be cured with the greatest of ease. I call forgiveness the one *quick fix* I believe in, and it is this *quick fix* which can relieve you of the burden and impeding nature of hatred. We are in the business of bringing success into our lives in increasing quantities; this involves some transient sacrifice, yet at times what has the apparency of forfeit can actually be the caring side of egocentricity. Forgiveness is both selfish for the instigator, and propitious to the beneficiary and humanity as a whole. This is why I extoll it as a practical virtue, and in this act I am certainly not unique. In the past I would have placed forgiveness before the concept of unconditional love as part of the process I call *gradual graduation.* For this book I have placed it afterwards, making unconditional love the aspiration, and forgiveness a humble, facilitating tool. This status does not undermine its power however!

Hatred has been a byword for the astrological age which has dominated us with Piscean energies for the past two thousand years. In recent history it has stimulated two world wars and caused untold human suffering and misery. It is a concept frequently traded on by the dark forces operating amongst the cover of mankind, along with mistrust, egotism, suspicion, cruelty, selfish power, misanthropy and separateness. Hatred is an adversary of evolution and it is impossible to be truly successful whilst harbouring this negative trait. Of course it is also the opposite to love, in both definition and physical feeling.

When you are depressed, if ever, and you make the effort to smile, no matter how forced or false that grin may be, the physiological reaction to that deed, is a rising of the spirits. It is something you just have to do, and through performing the action you are then helped by the physiological reaction. You can try this anytime you are feeling a little low ... it is similar to the results obtained by walking with a straight back, sitting upright in a chair, or inhaling cool and fresh air deeply into your lungs. It just works!

The relationship of forgiveness to hatred is similar. The impulse to forgive may be so slight as to be in danger of going unnoticed. If you pounce on the opportunity however, your impulse will be rewarded not in ratio; rather, by a more than threefold increase in the *Attention Units*, or AUs, which then become available to you for an assault on personal success. AUs found in the hatred, *AUs caught up in ignorance, AUs utilised in creating destructive plans, AUs caught in the crossover referencing of one hatred to another, AUs keeping you informed of who you are not speaking to ... who to ignore ... who to destroy by rumour ...* well, the list goes on, but I have outlined this negativity enough to draw positive attention to its drawbacks.

Now for a PAC Alchemy Nostrum ... it is impossible to hate and love at the same time. The law of opposites places these two harmonics of the same quality category at alternate ends of a linear concept. Similar attention unit types are utilised for both outlooks, and the power of the universe is at the disposal of any person who utilises the natural law which allows these harmonics to be turned into each other ... preferably a one way flow from hate to love!

Anyone can do this, but your ability in this endeavour will increase directly proportional to the amount of times you successfully practice, win and acknowledge yourself for doing so. The first step anyone must take in a true quest for success is a study of each concept that becomes available to them, then a choice between right and wrong, good and bad, fear and courage, up and down, back and forward and of course the matter in question, love and hate. In the preceding sentence you will find such examples all being opposite ends of each other and all following the same law that I have just described. You may therefore channel the feeling of fear into courage, much as you do with love into hate. This is an exciting field of endeavour, but it is with practical application that the actuality of my postulate, which I learnt through Hermetic Philosophy written by Three Initiates in a book called *The Kybalion*, comes alive and finds a beneficial place in your life.

♪

Play your favourite relaxing instrumental music at a low volume in the background. If you are unfamiliar with any particular piece, you may like to try one of my favourites ... Grieg's *Peer Gynt Suite*.

✎

Find a place in your exercise book where two blank pages face each other. On the left hand page, make a list of hates that are part of your life. This left hand page can be symbolic of the place that hate finds for itself on the left hand path. Be honest and search deeply ... you are the only person who will see this list. Use the word hate to precede

73

the object of negativity.

I hate ...

Utilise the initial impulse and write down whatever or whoever comes into your thoughts. What tends to happen is that as you think about a particular hatred, the emotion is not so strong as it is when coming involuntarily into your mind as a restimulated emotion. Understand this and do not go off at a tangent with thoughts like, *well I don't really hate ... dislike would be a better description ... I couldn't care less actually.* Let's get that hatred written down. Then, we put on our Advanced PAC Practitioner Hat labelled *Modern Alchemist.* We can now work a little white magic by transmuting hatred into love. On the right hand page, jot down the things you like about each noted hatred. Do not cringe. There is something likeable about even the most miserable examples of anything. Remember the inspiring example of Jesus Christ ... as he and his disciples passed the rotting corpse of a dead dog, they moaned about the stench and ugliness of the sight; He commented that its teeth were like pearls. Sometimes you have to be a little inventive, by saying things like, *I could like him if only he'd ...* even though this is a value judgement type approach which is normally frowned upon, we can take this route if it gets us to the other side ... *The Right Side.* Now, on the following clean facing pages, using the right hand sheet, write down the words *I love ...* followed by whoever or whatever you hated on the previous pages. Just do it! Nurture every possible like, good feeling, mental smile and wholesome thought you can muster about the previous hatred; that is the last time we will use this word.

I call this process ... *Positivitising the negative!*

❂

Feel the lightness of faster love vibrations and make a

74

decision to aspire in their direction ...

every day in every way
in all I do and all I say
I pledge myself to this intent
a life of love
wisely spent!

†

Write a letter to someone from your list, and without reference to anything in the past, communicate to them in a way that is real for your relationship. There must be an absence of ulterior motive, except the desire to flow love. Make a telephone call to someone that you ceased speaking to, and, speaking only in positives, outline a plan for the flourishing of your relationship.
Visit a friend whom you are no longer in contact with.
Do something you didn't like doing.
Mentally forgive yourself, your Parents, your friends, your enemies and your environment. If this is more than you can comfortably do at this time, at least send the communication in thought, telepathically. You will still benefit, and you may see some surprises bestowed upon the recipient as well as yourself. This method works in some cases even better than a direct contact between personalities!

Let's move on ...

Synthesis

It will be apparent as we travel this journey en route to success, that no single ingredient is the magic one. There *is* a lone panacea waiting in the wings, and I have described it as the Friendliest Force which is Love. We are only able to touch this concept in our own very human way, and it is through a synthesis of various positive means that we will discover our objective of success.

Most people seek happiness, and it is the single most listed goal in the world of personal development. It is only achievable whilst executing an otherwise unrelated aspiration. It is a human emotion closely allied to personality type traits and the astral plane of desire ... *success is getting what you want; happiness is wanting what you got.* Peace would be a more soulful quality to aim for, and serenity would be an ultimate. All of these abstracts that I mention, require the experience of synthesised knowledge.

It is through synthesis that the wonder of our brain really shows its true worth. The computing capacity of the brain as a servant of the mind, is so powerful that it is able to take many pieces of data and present them for your inspection in various different ways; it allows you a physical vision of the dense plane via the eyes; it computes your auditory capacity; it makes sense of your perceptions by translating its input into information chunks which can then be re-presented to you in any number of ways; it is indeed a great, yet much maligned gift.

Some religious camps relegate the brain, and indeed anything physical to the realms of *barely tolerable*. I read in an article promoted by a religious cult, about a railway worker who was involved in an accident. A steel crowbar smashed through his head; in at one side and out of the other. He apparently returned to work after minor surgery and with little interruption to his normal routine of mental and physical workings. The apparent happening was reported by the cult as supportive of their particular disregard for the physical brain. This specific cult makes unrealistic claims about their facility to aid the achievement of utopian states here and now ... after payment of an absurd amount of money. This perverse use of spiritual claims for financial reward appeals mainly to the personality; but nevertheless is damaging, and indeed keeps many from the Path for lifetime after lifetime. They have a different reality of the brain to the one which I value!

76

The quality of the physical vehicle is of paramount importance ... brain included ... and an understanding of synthesis is desirable if you are to be more in control of your assault on success. The word means literally, *the building up of a complex whole by the union of elements*. You are of course, the most magnificent example of synthesis that we are currently aware of. The human being is the only life form in which is found both *individual* spirit, or ego, and matter. It is this exact point that is the cause of a natural friction, evident in this blend of spirit and matter, and easily demonstrated by the fact that a human being will still be tired after a given number of hours of apparently doing nothing. The interaction of the two opposites is the cause, and sleep is the necessary effect. The group spirit of plants and animals will to a lesser extent produce similar phenomena, although much diluted.

Utilising our microcosmic application of the macrocosm phenomenon for individual and group gain, we must look at Nature's Will as is clearly visible in our environment. The tendency is towards blending, harmony and interdependence; where the minerals serve the plants, which in turn feed the animals, who so often serve humanity. Trees are the lungs of the planet; they breathe in our waste product of carbon dioxide, and in return for the gift and according to natural law, they provide us with a conversion of that gas into one which is essential for our existence ... *oxygen* ... the single most important element from a human body survival point of view.

Food chains illustrating a gradient eating process from the amoeba to the human are evidence of interdependence, although not an example I would wish to utilise in the dissemination of this PAC policy for humanity. You can look around and see many examples of the synthesising aspects of nature. The tendency is towards fusion ... as I have hinted ... we will always follow the universal example ... I postulate in line with greater teachings, that our ultimate goal is the merging back into a single spiritual unit which we can call God, Nature, The Infinite or any of the many other names that exist for the *perhaps* ultimate phenomenon; we can see the lower workings of this postulate by our tendency to gather together, to herd, to group into cities and to amalgamate.

The United Nations is an exciting and broader example of this curiosity. The European Economic Community illustrates the workings of *currently* twelve member states, and their aspiration, *or not*, of being one. The United States, along with many worldwide confederations can be taken as examples of the tendency to blend that is inherent and currently surfacing as an inclination in the more advanced of the human races. Let us not forget that some states are in the process of separating from *forced* ties also, but it is my belief that each new individualised state will begin the process of interdepending just as soon as its *will* has been stated and its status acknowledged.

For Humanity, and in any quest for success, it is important to note natural trends and try as much as possible to co-operate with them to a greater extent than has up until now been advisable. The human is in this unique position of gathering experience as a *being*, operating in the dense, material world of matter.

We must synthesise all that is good into a more creative whole.

This is co-operating with The Plan as I understand it. If we blend our inherent spirituality into the rough and tumble world of the physical universe, the end product will always be success, providing you are firstly cognisant of the natural laws that prevail. For instance, it would do no one any good at all if you were to attempt the instillation of divine values into the morays of a man who has drunk six litres of strong German beer, and is insisting that the only way to settle an argument is with a fight. Chances are you would get hit, and perhaps even laughed at by any onlookers. Stay clear of such situations and remember my rule of *gradual graduation*, which is derived from higher life; The Lord of the World talks to Shamballa ... word is passed on to the Hierarchy ... the Masters are then informed ... the Initiates get to know ... the Disciples are then told ... the Probationers learn of the concept ... the Aspirants are talked to ... the Persons of good deed are informed, who then translate the message to the mass of humanity. Those responsible at each stage of the route, pour onto the words essential dilution that the concept be understood down the descending line.

There is a line of communication which can be lived in all aspects of life. The communication line is of paramount importance for the furtherance of the Evolutionary Plan. We can also see that it is vital for the smooth running of any operation. *Do not spread seed on infertile soil* and always apply what you learn gradually to your surroundings.

The brain is the tool of the mind within the cerebrum. In order for it to function effectively you must respect it biologically. It needs certain nourishment and would itself, naturally seek to avoid destructive drugs such as alcohol and nicotine; even caffeine and tannin. I am not telling you to abstain from these substances immediately ... *gradual graduation* applies to this situation also ... just be aware that if you are to mount a serious assault on success, such abstention will set you apart from the masses.

The cleverest trick that can be learnt from the macrocosmic phenomenon of synthesis, is that you should always blend every single aspect of each episode in all courses of action as an effort to facilitate ultimate success, which must be *the synthesis of all that is good into a more creative whole.*

✪

Define the word *alchemy* and ponder its usage within the concept of synthesis

♪

Listen to music by Bach, Beethoven, Chopin, Handel, or your favourite classical composer. Note the blending and harmony within their compositions, of much, into the greater whole.

🏃

Gather three quite diverse pieces of information, and synthesise them into a new and useful whole. Practice the end result!

We now move on to a discussion of rights and wrongs, ethics and morals, laws and justice, by suggesting, *let right be done* ...

let right be done

Guide Three

"Every Cause has its Effect; every Effect has it Cause; everything happens according to Law; Chance is but a name for Law not recognized; there are many planes of causation, but nothing escapes the Law." ... *The Kybalion*

Ethics

Please do not think for one moment that I have mixed a sacred tenet of *Ageless Wisdom* with a mundane tradition of the *British Judiciary System* by mistake, or for little reason. Study the title of *Guide Three* and afterwards contemplate the quote from *Hermetic Philosophy* which I found in *The Kybalion*.

It would be magnificent if *right was done* whenever a case was heard in court and this phrase has an interesting history. In common law, judges had to decide litigation on the basis of established laws or rules and not on the foundation of fairness. As a result, plaintiffs who felt they were not in receipt of justice, petitioned the King or Queen directly, as it was recognised that these Heads of State were the "fountains of justice"; *perhaps dating back unknowingly to the times when Kings were indeed godly, according to their spiritual endowment and presence as Divine Beings on earth*. At times, these petitions became too numerous for royalty to handle, and they would be referred to the Chancellor, who was usually both legally and clerically qualified ... sometimes known as the Keeper of the King's Conscience. Such a petition would start by stating ... *Let right be done* ... and the Chancellor would decide a case on conscience and natural justice, ignoring the formal rules of the common law.

It is this representation of law that interests me; of course it is only such interpretation that could perform any public duty for both plaintiffs and defendants, *according to the natural law of*

Karma. Unfortunately, there are few people in power capable of natural judgement, without referring to their own personalities and the intrinsic inconsistencies that inevitably must be found there.

We find ourselves more often than is comfortable, in the position of allowing criminals to escape punishment, on technicalities inherent in criminal laws which are supposed to be there for the protection of the innocent and correction of the guilty. I am afraid that law as we know it within the system, cannot be a guideline of any description for our interpretation of ethics. Of course you must stay within its boundaries if you are to freely operate within society, but the law can so often be used to justify a wrong action. *I am within my rights ... the rules say ... Judge So and So said that it was okay ... the law states quite clearly ...* no, I am afraid that a true attempt at full success must harbour an *intuitional ethical code* at the core of its basic impulse. You must be propelled by inspiration achieved through a fully cognisant usage of inner rights and wrongs.

You would be within the boundaries of law if you capriciously killed a pigeon ... does that make such action defensible? You would remain unpunished should gain be forthcoming through certain sharp practices ... omitting to tell a potential purchaser of a house that its roof leaks, the central heating system is inefficient and there is no mains drainage. *You should have discovered these shortcomings for yourself,* is the frequent rejoinder when defects are discovered in such situations. *Caveat Emptor,* as the Latin saying goes ... let the buyer beware.

You cannot ever incur long term gains from an action which entails someone else losing!

I utilise my *Win For All* magic ingredient whenever I engage in business. This concept is self explanatory ... *win for all or no deal!* It is quite simple, with no bad karmic consequences for me. A selfish action has gains inherently built into it for all involved to be happy, when utilising this magic PAC alchemical ingredient. You need never wonder if a potential deal is right or wrong; just ask yourself the question, *does anyone lose if we continue by consummating this deal?* If the answer is yes, then walk away from temptation ... whatever you think could be gained, will be taken away from you no matter how much you justify a short term action to yourself.

The law of Karma is intrinsically within you ... it is not imposed by some great anthropomorphic being in the Heavens looking out for wayward strays with a view to punishment. Just as you are an indivisible part of the universe to which we all belong, so too is your subliminal consciousness linked to cosmic life, *as a microcosm of it.*

I didn't just blindly accept karmic consequence as a principle before absorbing it in my modus operandi ... I looked around at people I knew and saw both good and bad in lives that were superficially and socially content. I had a friend whose every word was critical and destructive ... he was fun in a very narrow sense of the word, but appealed to only the most basic of instincts. He took great delight in the accumulation of money, which superficially I had no objection to; it wasn't until I examined some consequences of his every day actions that I found it necessary, *though outside the limits of my normal demeanor*, to discuss his behaviour with him. He actually left a trail of misery behind him ... his karma was bodily visible ... he was greatly overweight ... had difficulty breathing ... was always involved in I win you lose deals ... had no true friends ... no good intentions ... and *his greatest difficulty was in spending any of the money that he had accumulated!* According to another universal law which states that *nothing remains the same*, he had been deteriorating since *before* the moment I had met him.

Why was I a friend in the first place? It was a mistake, but once committed I did as much as I felt was necessary to illustrate the effect he was having on the world ... he paid lip service to the subject of possible self improvement, but the deterioration continued and I knew that he was very likely laughing behind my back as he continued karmically deteriorating, whilst holding on to his old habits. I relate this anecdote because it is both relevant as an example of what to avoid, and to show, if already involved, how to extricate yourself from a difficult existing situation. I ceased all communication with this person, as he was a negative influence on my life!

Does anyone affect you in this way?

We must remember that karma is *totally* operational on the *complete* spectrum between the opposites of good and bad.

SK

Man! This is a sticky wicket! In all the studies that I have undertaken, good explanations for these two opposites of good and bad have always alluded me; until recently that is, and with the help of more than a little enlightenment from Patti. (Patricia Diane Cota-Robles) She gave me a real simple way to define these two ever present qualities ... if it is in harmony with The Divine Plan then it is good; disharmony is bad, evil and in fact, causes the illusion you mention in this book of the psychic astral plane. This is also known as Maya, which is a crystallized smog and that tunnel of darkness often perceived in near death experiences. It is the realm of earth-bound spirits, and exists only in the mental realm of humanity ... and can ONLY be transmuted by Forgiveness back into its original Divine Harmonious Light, which is the complete purpose of the Silent Knight philosophy.
... *end of note.*

Karma does not therefore only produce negative consequences; positive reverberations will also be enjoyed as a measure, and evidence of pure outflow. I have other friends, students of karmic workings, who habitually avoid any situation which may place them in a position of having to render future amends for present gain. Others whom I know, are happy to live a normal life where they perform more right actions than they exhibit bad, totally ignorant of karmic law from a theosophical point of view, yet living a successful life within karma's positive boundaries.

Karma cannot be manipulated ... it is as natural as the tides and ever present as our sun. Perhaps, through spiritual progression, one may eventually be able to defer certain complications resultant from past endeavours, whilst performing a service for humanity; this service may be *self* accepted as the amends ... I cannot discuss this as my knowledge is too scant on the issue. All research that I have completed has pointed towards every Soul of whatever quality, being responsible under natural law for themselves. This does not include choosing your punishment and selecting particularly agreeable amends! This you may do on a conscious basis, but such action would bear little connection to the subliminal aspects of karma that I have discussed. Yet again, I refer you to the work of HP Blavatsky and Alice A Bailey for a substantial treatment of this topic, although many other sources have also covered some aspects of this vast philosophical body of natural law.

Living on this dense physical plane conditions us to look outward. The path towards the attainment of true success is so much easier for those of us willing to look inward and learn about the higher planes of existence. When exploring your inner worlds, the mind to which you are attached will be ever more apparent. Your choices will become easier as you have more of them to make.

As a subject, ethics are inextricably linked to the workings of karma, and it is through the mind that you will conquer the obstacles that stand on the path leading to your very own win for all ingredients. This is a quote from a translation of the Bhagavad-Gita ... *For him who has conquered the mind, the mind is the best of friends; but for one who has failed to do so, his mind will remain the greatest enemy* ... more words of wisdom from ancient teachings. What will you do with them?

Make a list of traits which could be leading you astray from your route towards personal success. Include *I win you lose ... you lose I win ... I lose you lose* situations. Note down anyone in your sphere of activity who makes you feel negative, and determine the reason and subsequent consequence.

Illuminate a concept, by defining two words using a good dictionary ... *Macrocosm* and *Microcosm*. Can we be smaller duplications of a larger whole? Are we as cyclical as the cosmos? Do you feel a relationship between yourself and the universe? Ponder the significance of karma and determine if your life is to be self regulatory in the future.

Without creating unnecessary havoc in your life, undo one wrong that you have been responsible for, and create in writing a new ethical policy with your inner guidance system as its counselling force. This may change as your life progresses, but will nevertheless provide you with a stepping stone towards more power.

The Advanced PAC Table of Seven Ethical States
Power

Every aspect of your life is aligned. You are actively working towards the accomplishment of known goals, and are thus constantly in a state of happiness, which at times may not be outwardly apparent. Your money supply is adequate, your surroundings are harmonious with your spiritual functioning, and you are cognisant of universal laws and their effects. People like you ... you like people. Love underlies all that you contemplate. Service is a pleasurable aspect of your outflows, and giving has long taken precedence over taking. You always take time to meditate, and treat your inner worlds as superior to that which is physically tangible to the majority. *Everything outwardly visible, was firstly created within,* is a maxim which guides your life. You have transcended the quality of life enjoyed by Advanced PAC Practitioners, and understand just how important guiding PAC principles were in your ascent of the Path which leads upward ever. You are in fact, a *PAC Transcendee.*

Knowing

You are in possession of much knowledge, and it is for this reason that you are operating within a structure of the ethical department called *knowing.* All of your wisdom does not manifest into your life as physical action, but you are a good person with high aspirations. Most of what you touch is beneficent of this contact, and you pay homage to the inner worlds without spending, what is to you, unnecessary time exploring *what you already know.* You are an Advanced PAC Practitioner, and acknowledged within your field of operation as efficient and desirable. You understand the *win for all* ingredient, but you are still under the illusion that it is not possible to attain its inclusion in everything that you do. You are capable of walking away from selfish short term gain, and indeed, understand the implications were you to indulge in its temptation.

Operating

You have completed an apprenticeship in the finer points of life with a positive attitude, as a PAC Practitioner. You know that *energy always follows thought,* and you therefore think, then outflow much effort and cherish subsequent achievement. Your surroundings do not always live up to your expectations, and mild irritability creeps into your life through the back door. Indulgence in temptation is less regular than your adherence to the PAC ethical code; you outflow love and expect its return. You are a good manager, who lives mainly in the outer world, yet knows the value of inner exploration, but are too busy to practice it.

Balanced

An equal amount of everything sums up this state of conduct, although the life will always fall towards the positive and avoid the ultimate negatives. Good and poor; love and dislike; knowing and not sure; courageous and holding back, are all differentials which can be experienced at this level. Certainty is frequently experienced, although it is present as a physical intelligence rather than an inner knowing. The conscience is active and prevents excesses. Possessions are treasured as commensuration for hard won knowledge and physical effort. Love is an emotion often connected to sex. The ethical code has almost as many don'ts as it does do's. You sometimes get angry out of proportion to the stimulation from your target.

Coping

You get by ... how? ... you are not quite sure! Without some of the automaticities of life you would be dead. You could be an opportunist thief, but would never steal from someone who would suffer as a consequence. The *short sharp* shock syndrome of punishment appeals to your sense of right and wrong, and you do your best to avoid detection as a *below par operator* in life. Your best chance of accomplishment is winning the pools, but your karma will only allow this to happen as perverse punishment.

Liability

Take what you can ... cheat off early ... give nothing and moan! The carpers and criticisers who contribute nothing to the world are in this ethical band. Untrustworthy, uncommitted, indecisive, underhand, under everything and ultimately unclean. The chances of rising from this level in one lifetime are slim and unusual. They need a helping hand in keeping with their outlook on others, with an additional portion of the love flow which cannot be an outflow from them. They will take advantage and this should be noted if such people are in your vicinity.

Repressive

People operating at the bottom end of the ethical table are called repressive because they stop others. These lives can have the apparency of functioning in any band up to *knowing,* but they have no idea how it really feels to be any way other than how they actually are. The stopping of others is the most despicable act that can be contemplated, yet there are many people who do this. There are however, few who actually live their lives with stopping as their operation base. Every gain that is visible in another, is a threat to the repressive. They are nervous in the presence of creation, and very covert in their operation to stop it. I doubt you will ever detect a true repressive, as, figuratively speaking, *they only come out at night* ... you may though, and if you do, using words of advice similar to those given Alice Bailey by her then superior when she was continuously verbally abused by someone she was trying to help in her earlier days ... leave that one for God!

All life forms are engaged in the common activity we call

survival, and one aspect of it is being *right*. At this level I call Repressive, being right for such people is attained by the process of *elimination*. If they can make everyone else *wrong*, then the only ones left to be *right* are them! Makes *crazy* sense doesn t it?

Morals

... and how are they different to ethics? I differentiate by affording ethics a more active concept, whereas I feel that morals are inclined towards the inward mechanisms. What comes into my mind when I think of this word is ...

to be in tune with your own conscience!

Rights and wrongs are not all standard, nor will they ever be. Certain basic truths remain fairly constant, but even in matters which seem cut, dried and above inspection, curves can be introduced to make a person re-think their outlooks. Killing another human being seems to be an ultimate inviolable area, yet, and as this book professes to be a practical volume, we have to accept that in unusual circumstances it may be necessary to kill. *It would be ludicrously pedantic to claim otherwise.* If a murderer was holding a knife to the throat of your child, threatening to kill him or her, and you had a gun trained on the killers temple would you not shoot?

Does this mean that human life is only sacrosanctish?

Of course not, we must always remember that absolutes do not exist. They apparently exist only as concepts in our minds, with the knowledge that to us humans, they are in fact unattainable. *To the degree that they are unattainable,* must not make this fact an excuse for mediocrity or inaccuracy. It must also be noted that different societies have a variety of morays which are consequent upon their morals.

I remember during the Gulf War of 1990, whilst we were pondering the rights and wrongs of our actions in liberating Kuwait from the invasion by Iraq, it was reported by a Baghdad newspaper that a new gadget had just been devised for the efficient amputation of fingers from the hands of thieves. This method of applying punishment can be offensive to western thought patterns, but the Iraqis, and other middle eastern countries, swear by it as an excellent preventative measure against theft.

Domestic dogs are eaten in Korea and the Philippines ... *the subject of many a Joan Rivers joke!*

Marriages are arranged by many Indian families. Female circumcision has been performed on more than one billion women throughout the world! In case you are unfamiliar with this particular encroachment on freedom, it entails cutting off the clitoris, or at least sowing the surrounding flesh over it, thus making smaller the adjacent orifice and removing the potential for pleasurable sensation and stimulation in that area, *on babies and young girls!*

One billion females!

I think we have enough examples to work with. We can see the danger of morals as a mode of law. Many doctors performing female circumcision, feel they are exercising a service in following tradition. Many Harley Street doctors feel they are performing a more valuable service by undoing, *when this is clinically and fiscally possible,* the barbaric act of this circumcision.

The west judges Koreans and the Filipinos to be backward in their eating of dogs ... just as vegans and vegetarians *feel about meat eaters in general!* When we criticise those countries practicing the amputation of digits as punishment ... *they laugh at our rising levels of crime!* Animal lovers would not dream of harming a cow in a field, yet they would not flinch at it being *killed by proxy* for them, preferably somewhere out of sight, by a butcher! They can then buy it as a sanitised package in the supermarket, or order it medium rare in a restaurant, without regard to the history of the meal.

A society is as healthy as it does not need rules and regulations, and it will be found, if you care to examine this area, that those countries steeped in petty legislation and feeble by-laws, are strangled by an abundance of lower band inhabitants, and that it is just these people who have necessitated such bars to personal expression for everyone else. This is a fact that must be accepted and worked around.

If there is any striving to do, it must be in the area of increasing awareness of general principles within the spiritual subject of life. As this type of awareness rises, so will instances decrease of abhorrence towards the actions of a neighbour. If there were no theft there would be no punishment. An absence of conscience on the part of doctors allows the continuance of female circumcision ... an increase in awareness will handle this simple defect of character. Dogs have the same rights as all animals. If we are educated to the level of cognisance on this basic issue, we will cease eating all meat.

The purpose of this next exercise is to increase awareness and encourage personal choice, in a moral way.

❁

Ponder the word conscience ... an inner balance of what is right and wrong *to you!* Compare your feelings about conscience to the table of ethics found earlier in guide three.

🚶

Observe your friends and colleagues. Note their

interpretations of right and wrong. How do their outlooks impact their personal lives?

Make a list of seven events that occur or have occurred in your general sphere of awareness. Note down your moral verdict next to each, and then further note any conclusions you are aware of that have been formulated by others, and which are at variance with yours.

Play your favourite instrumental music, and *Grant Spiritual Beingness* to all antagonism whilst listening. This means allowing and permitting all aspects of everyone ... *to be!*

Laws

From 1976 until 1994, I believed that man was as great as he was able to change his environment to suit himself. I extracted many selfish angles from much of the philosophy which I studied, and did not afford our planet the status of life. I was contemptuous of anything physical, including the human body, and very single minded about getting my own way as a right. The main missing ingredient from all of my studies was *love,* which I call *The Friendliest Force.* It was most fortunate that I attracted the *love catalyser* for all my knowledge, in the January of 1994, as I believe that this knowledge would be virtually useless or at the very worst dangerous, without this missing link.

The basic law is ... The Friendliest Force which is Love!

This *love catalsyer* was introduced into my life through my first book, and a letter from a storyteller in Belgium who had bought and read it. Just before the Christmas of 1993, this person wrote to me and asked what made the PAC different from all the other *come and go* groups that he had encountered in his life of mainly esoteric experience. I replied that it was up to the members to keep the group in existence and dictate direction, and that I was merely the instrument. He telephoned a reply and said that he was often in our vicinity *on business,* and that he would attend the following meeting, which was to be in the January of 1994. At that Gathering, and after I had talked about a variety of books which I was recommending to the PAC, I invited my new friend to speak, which he did.

He told us a simple yet spellbinding story of mystical content, which re-awakened the love spark within me. I had spent many years nurturing the quality of affinity, whilst suppressing the superior flow of love. His story touched myself and many others that evening, and he continues to be involved with the PAC in a variety of ways. As the love spark was rekindled, so too was my attention directed toward studies in keeping with this new driving force, which demanded to be unleashed.

Without love, the universe would simply fall apart. An absence of love disintegrates creation, and it is artists and creators that make an otherwise uninviting environment, tantalisingly tempting to the spirit. A society is as great as it has artists and creative people in it, and it is the greatest folly to make any circumstances disagreeable or hostile to such people.

Let me be clear that this love of which I talk has no relationship whatsoever to sex, and the platitudes which now freely use the word to confer grandeur on otherwise mundane aspects of life ... *I just love that car ... I love eating ... people love this or that ... love means never having to say you are sorry ...* I relate these platitudinous irrelevancies to egoism.

A more accurate description of the basic law is ...

The Friendliest Force which is Altruism!

Love has lost its meaning as an outflow in the everyday sense, yet I believe that deep down it still has an impact as the most beautiful of concepts. We merely have to remind ourselves of love as an outflow, and its meaning returns to our mental lexicon with the greatest of ease. John Lennon communicated about the law of love in his 1973 song *Mind Games,* when he simply stated ... *love is the answer.* I cannot say if he knew just how near the truth he was with this universal antidote, but something tells me he had a fair idea, and certainly a beautiful way of stating it.

So, as love is the basic law, what does this reveal to us as an aid to personal success? It tells us that any quality other than altruism, utilised or displayed as a carrier wave for communications or actions, is merely aberration, *which is a departure from rationality.* A mark of true PAC Practitionership is the ability to inject this basic law into every aspect of ones life. This is one of those concepts that leans towards the pedantic, until you get into action and discover the power of love for yourself .

Love heals, coheres, harmonises, liberates, cleanses, tones and builds ... it smiles, gives, and accepts the return fully cognisant of the edict which states that you get what you give ... *to give what you get is the exact opposite of a major dictate for happy living!* Happiness is a loving feeling, joy is related, gladness is a cousin, bliss is the elder of the tribe. Serenity and inspiration are rewards which are truly worthy of aspiration towards a honing of the skills which make love stay to the forefront of our meditations.

All other laws are merely supportive of love, and exist to prevent any other human emotion taking hold and elevating the darker side of human nature into a position of dominance. If this law of love is so powerful, how can it be so easily overtaken by human failings of hate, jealousy, envy and desire? Love is a universal law and not an individual beingness. We mainly have freedom of choice in all that we say or do ... this cannot be prevented even by the more powerful ubiquitous forces ... this itself is a law known as *The Law of Allowances*. We can be indirectly guided, but no one person has the right to interfere with the individual karmic wheel of another. We are all at different levels of awareness, and most of us still live in the desire world of the astral plane a good deal of the time. How many of us are able to sit quietly in an uninterruptable situation, and dispatch waves of thought forms containing unconditional love and forgiveness. This is the action of a Silent Knight. The power of this vibrational type is the mental stuff that dissipates the clouds of aberrative desire stuff that surround this planet. There are human beings working night and day doing just this one unselfish act of unconditional altruism.

The fresh energy which is rapidly becoming increasingly available to us in this new age of Aquarius, cannot be enjoyed to its fullest capacity and consequent maximum benefit, whilst this gargantuan cloud of uncontrolled babble, and chaotic desire for selves, remains in its present foremost position. We afford the world of desire a greater relevance in our lives, than the finer aspects of the abstract world which can be experienced in mental realms.

Perhaps this new energy is the re-appearance of the Christ as a principle. Can you imagine how difficult and, not to mention, uncomfortable it would be, for someone like the Christ, living a high quality existence, vibrating at such a speed, to come into contact with gross denseness. High quality spiritual energy solidifies when it comes into contact with low band thought values. We must increase the planetary vibration that we may encourage contact with higher spiritual energies. I need only remind you in a very physical way, how you may feel if a stinking inebriated tramp were to manifest in your midst and begin to exert his or her expectations of life onto you. *You would cry out for help!*

Justice

I believe that Justice is a balancing act!

The symbol for Justice in or over most courthouses in the United States of America is a beautiful woman holding a balance and wearing a blindfold ... signifying perhaps, *blind* weighing of evidence; that is, no hearsay ... only facts in the balance. It is also the astrological sign for Libra *the balancing point* ... the half-way stage around the Zodiac.

Picture a pair of scales ... when they are horizontal, the balance of justice has been achieved. Up or down signifies injustice, either to your benefit or loss ... whichever, it is of nothing but transient and illusory benefit or loss to you, and my advice is to balance the scales at your earliest convenience.

Temptation can often manifest, suggesting that you take selfish advantage of a certain situation, as a positive swing of the pendulum making amends for a negative swing from the past ... *don't!* Let it pass and await the imminent swing that will arrive without harming others.

If you don t want anyone to know it, don't do it, states the wise old saying!

There are many different levels of justice, from cosmic and planetary scenarios down to the humblest insect. From a human point of view, we refer to the courts for justice, but it has been found time after time that truth is often hard to come by in these places, causing juries to sometimes be defined as ... *twelve people deciding who has the best attorney!*

If you demand justice from within yourself, it will eventually be found constantly manifesting itself into every day life. It may take some time to clean the slate if your past is littered with injustice you may have inflicted on others, but it is nevertheless an activity that must be started before the results can be enjoyed to their fullest. Much as alcoholics must refuse their first drink and smokers will stub out their last cigarette, before the benefits of abstinence can be evident, so must we all stop any internal cycles of action which may be causing us to precipitate injustice on our surroundings.

𝄞

Play your favourite music ... smile ... and recite the affirmation *Honesty is my Power!* until you feel comfortable with the concept.

Let us now turn our attention to a treatment of communication ...

communication

I will speak ill of no man, and speak all the good I know about everybody ... *Benjamin Franklin*

Self

I made a thorough search of my esoteric literature for a clever quote to head this fourth section, and I am afraid that no relevant *spirit-jogging phrase* was forthcoming. I then set eyes on a very old version of the 1938 book which I have already mentioned, by Dale Carnegie, called *How to Win Friends and Influence People*. The butt of many a cheap sit-com joke, this book is an outstanding example from the thirties surge in personal development literature, which later came to be included in what is called the *Human Potential Movement*.

✎

Begin, or continue to compile a list of books which will aid your quest for success, and add this one to both it, and your collection, as soon as possible.

The sight of this book gladdened my eyes as I remembered just how valuable it had been to me during my earlier excursions into *The World of Personal Development*. My joy very nearly turned into dismay when the thought crossed my mind that perhaps I should merely point readers in the direction of this one book to cover the whole subject of communication ... now that I am composed I realise that there is far more scope for writing on this topic than is already provided for us in other works. I therefore offer you these following words on communication, and stress that this subject perhaps comprises the most important aspect of the universes in which we live ... both subjective and objective.

I also remembered that I had actually taken a *Communication*

Course many years ago, and on reflection it seemed so different to the subject matter offered by Dale Carnegie. Once again a blend of wisdom from many sources will mould the key which will unlock potential hidden behind any surface inabilities you may have in this essential subject of Communication.

One of the very first phrases I utilised, and still do, as a communication affirmation, was the first portion of the quote which heads this guide ... *I will speak ill of no man* ... I would openly recite it at people to whom I was just about to impart yet another devious set of words designed to destroy some mutual acquaintance usually not then present. This phrase would stop me indulging in old destructive habits, often producing a cognisant smile in the recipient.

You see, unfortunately I made a name for myself quite early in life, as *a clever lad with words*. I enjoyed the acclaim and began to specialise in verbal destruction, skillfully defended when criticism of my habit was forthcoming, behind the platitude that *words don't hurt,* which of course they can.

From the *Ageless Wisdom,* I learned just how valuable the throat centre is to our progress as human beings along the evolutionary track. It is the larynx which sets us apart from our animal associates, who obviously are not so far advanced along their own Path as we are on ours. A book called *Human Destiny* written by Lecomte du Noüy, eloquently illustrated with words just how important our abilities in this field really are. I no longer have this book otherwise I would quote verbatim ... in a nutshell of my own words then ...

The illustration concerns chickens and just how long it would take them to learn the dangers of crossing a road. They would learn by *genetic imprint* after an exceedingly long period of time, and by trial and error, that the chances of death were indeed too great to contemplate crossing the road. They would not know why they did not cross ... it would merely be a stimulus response mechanism ... *does the name Pavlov ring a bell?*

It would perhaps take up to one million years for the encodement of this information into the genes to occur. Many chickens would be killed before a mother chicken would be stimulated to obstruct the path of her offspring as they tried to cross. Eventually the genetic imprint in the young chicks would be strong enough to prevent crossing without external stimuli from the mother.

How do we human beings learn? It takes less than a minute to tell a child this information in a classroom ... *if you cross that road you may be killed ... don't cross it without help, until you are older and able to do so on your own!*

That illustrates a value of the larynx!

The area in which the larynx is found is also a chakra called the throat centre. Remember this is the centre of *will* power, decision and God's Will. As I mentioned earlier, these chakras channel cosmic energy through the etheric body, and step this energy down into a suitable form for utilisation by the physical vehicle. One of our goals in personal development is to raise the grade of our aspirations, and as we do this, our attention also rises from the lower regions of our bodies upward. As attention transfers from the solar plexus regions, it passes through the heart centre and finds its way to the throat centre, before hopefully travelling to the crown centre, with perhaps many intermittent stops in other centres, along the way.

With etheric energy centred in the throat region, we become creative in this area, just as the lower regions produce lesser creativity of maybe a sexual character for example. Verbal creativity is of a higher nature and certainly worthy of aspiration. Even though the impetus for spoken communication comes from a thought form not necessarily generated in this throat area; it is development of this region which will promote best utilisation of the benefits which it can bestow upon the strivings for success of any individual.

How do we transfer energy and attention upward from the lower to the higher regions. One way is to live an ethical and giving life which will help raise focus quite naturally, provided there is an aspiration to so do. Another is to concentrate attention on this task, and insist that your focus rises from the sexual areas, towards the love found in the heart area, onward to the throat and upward to the crown ... all the while retaining the qualities of the lower centres just transcended. Easier said than done, I hear you think! True! It is not the purpose of this book to dwell on centres, chakras or kundalini fire, and it is only when aims necessitate mention that I will include such information, albeit of a general nature.

Communication is an ability that is quickly mastered in its most basic forms, by personalities who utilise it in sales, television, radio and business, to *get what they want* from a given situation. It is one of the more tangible abstractions usually associated with learned people, yet easily mastered by lesser intellects ... *superficially!*

Real communication begins with understanding!

Your mental lexicon is an invaluable tool for this end and must be nurtured and routinely bolstered with additions of useful words. It is through verbal knowledge, that access is granted to the realms of greater concepts, and it is in these regions where you will discover a closer tie with your true self ... *the gnostic being.* Refuse to pass words that you do not understand, as to do so can lead to an undermining of confidence, so valuable in any quest for success.

In order to reach understanding, you must develop love, or simple affinity, for whatever or whoever it is you wish to communicate with. To omit this step is to render your words ineffective before they even leave your mouth ... or pen! Affinity should never be false or forced, and I guarantee that you need never lie about liking. There will always be some aspect of a person, however unreal this may at first seem, that you can like and develop affinity with ... *find that aspect and focus on it!*

Like everything in this universe, both a positive and a negative pole are needed for life; if we did not have our darker side comprising of more basic instinctual impulses, as well as our concept enjoying, creative, light and spiritual aspect, we would not be capable of consciousness on this physical plane. We can say that the animal part of us is negative and the spiritual aspect is positive. When seeking that facet within another that you can like, comprehension of the negative which is in all of us, can help divert attention to the spiritual and positive goodness that, have no doubt, will be present in no matter how small a quantity.

True communication between any two people must have as part of its carrier wave, a degree of reality. The amount of reality present within the communication will be in direct ratio to its effectiveness. You can have colleagues understand concepts quite unfamiliar to them under normal conditions, if you dress the carrier wave in a form which is familiar; this will transmute carrier wave reality into understanding of an otherwise incomprehensible concept. Allegories, analogies, and metaphors are excellent examples of this theory in action.

Make a list of three communication problems that you have experienced recently. Read over what you have written and decide to improve on one episode. Write in allegorical form, perhaps utilising analogies, an explanation quite unrelated to the actual content you wish to transmit. At he end of your story, *make the point!*

Get into action by communicating allegorically, that which you were unable to transmit ordinarily. Note the result and hone the rough edges. Remember a*llegory power* and consider its inclusion in your future modus operandi.

Affinity blended with reality, will inject understanding into your communications. Love fused with authenticity, will always render potent, whatever communication skills may have been nurtured be an ndividual!

Self and others
How do you handle communication delivered to you in an unpalatable fashion?

You have a number of choices: You can walk away from it ... argue with it ... reason with it ... plead with it ... submit to it ... or ... *dominate it!*

There is nothing wrong with using this word domination ... you can dominate whilst still granting someone space to be themselves. Of course, your motivation must be honourable if you are to pursue this course of action; I feel that you will have cognited on many new concepts so far in your reading of this book, and I for one have no doubts about the rights and wrongs of intention, as well as the repercussions of ill feeling.

To help any doubters, some ageless wisdom in the form of three lines from the *Tao Te Ching;* in English, *The Book of the Way,* by the Chinese mystic and sage Lao Tzu.

Those who would take over the earth
And shape it to their will
Never, I notice, succeed.

As with all facets of true personal development, it is the blending of aspects that will light the way to alchemical success. A beneficial social intercourse between any two people must contain satisfaction for each. Domination utilised for this end is not only honourable ... it is highly desirable and needs to be practiced.

Too many people are unable to steer even their own communications in any satisfactory direction. *Going off the point* is the most frequent irritant ... *being unspecific is another* ... *inaccuracy ... falseness ... lack of clarity ... uncouthness ... constant trivial jokeyness and lack of substance,* are others. Let us not forget also, a lack of acknowledgement, which is a silent demonstration of inattention and rude disinterest. I witness this shortcoming frequently in many varied aspects of life.

Communication domination is PAC Magic in a most tangible form. All Advanced PAC Practitioners utilise it, and the most skillful actually instill in the recipient a feeling of accomplishment.

The art is simply to keep someone to the point and extract from the communication exactly what it is that should be extracted; whether that something is for yourself or the other person. This involves practice in the adeptness of acknowledgement. This simple concept is one of the easiest to manage, yet powerful in its utilisation. Lack of acknowledgement can actually cause a physiological imbalance in a victim. You will all have episodes or acts from your past that you can recall, which you feel should have been acknowledged in some way, and were not.

One of the very first aspirations any success seeker should ponder is that ability to exist *without acknowledgement!* The very fact that acknowledgement is what most people desire in life, above all else, leads me to the simplistic conclusion that it is the first abstraction that needs to be dominated. You will transcend the need for acknowledgement ... by practice.

𝝠

Decide that you no longer need acknowledgement of any description!

1 Spend half an hour picking up litter in someone elses street, ensuring that no one notices you doing this.

2 Write a helpful letter to someone who is struggling to make a humanistic point that the majority of people have no time for. Sign it with your *pen name*.

3 Devote one meditation to peace, by flowing love and forgiveness to the most brutal killer that you are aware of.

4 If you are short of money, give some to a planetary aware charity. If you have enough money, acknowledge a source other than yourself as the provider of that wealth.

Tough eh?

Especially point number 3, which I actually realised through help gained at a London PAC Gathering, was an especially good service to perform. That dark side of humanity which is capable of killing a fellow traveller, lies within us all. As I have already mentioned, we inhabit a cosmos of duality. *Everything* comprises of two opposite poles. I venture to state that every one of us will have killed in some lifetime or other. The murderers of today are like the *you's* of yesterday? They manifest that which you may have already dominated. I do not excuse them ... they must do that themselves ... I merely point out an alternative viewpoint to the one exoterically available in many a newspaper headline.

Without the good people of this planet ... this planet would not be!

I encourage them as I do their darker counterparts. This is the only constructive way forward into the dawning of a vibrantly fresh tomorrow. Learn to deal with the darker side of humanity as a celebration of the negative pole which gives us consciousness on this physical plane of existence. How do we do that? Even though this professes to be a practical volume, its sphere of postulate does not extend to that particular remedy. It is for the relevant reformers to ponder, cognite and act with a less judgmental outlook on crime.

Through reflection on an angle of communication, we have encountered this challenge called *human acknowledgement*. The power harnessed within this subject became apparent to me, after I read of an experiment which was quickly discontinued when the forthcoming results caused death ... during the 1950s, a comparison was made between two different sets of newly born babies. The first set were cuddled, loved, spoken to, smiled at and cherished, whilst their mothers fed them. The other set were picked up by nurses, given their milk and placed back in their cots without a word spoken or a kindness flowed.

I am sure I need not relate the results of this heartless experiment ... you can guess that the loved babies flourished and the neglected babies withered ... what you may not have surmised is that *some of the neglected babies died* before the experiment could be discontinued.

The feeding was not acknowledgment enough, even though it would prevent prosecution if such a case ever entered the judiciary procedure. Acknowledgement works like magic, yet is simple to master. The following exercise is one of the few practical routines

111

in this book which requires another person to be included objectively rather than just as your subject. Who you choose is not important, provided they are cognisant of the rules ... *no value judgements ... no facial expressions ... no body language ... and eventually no irrelevant or stray thoughts.*

Sit opposite your partner, each holding any type of book or magazine from which you will both read. The first person will read one sentence from their publication. After it has been delivered and understood, following a relevant and polite but brief ommunication gap, an acknowledgement should be forthcoming. The type of acknowledgement will depend on the category of communication issued ... *I understand ... yes ... a smile... okay ... mm ... a nod of the head.* Do not forget the no value judgement rule, even if you disagree with what has been said. Alternate as presenter and recipient, between the two of you. Persevere with this routine and you will soon get used to accepting and delivering any type of communication without ever being waylaid. This exercise will also pave the way for one which follows soon. Good communicators are always, and will forever be, in demand. Spend some time in this area of personal development and you will soon discover uninvited benefits creeping in amongst old and worn out habits.

Public speaking

If you have no desire whatsoever at any time in your life to speak in public, this section still applies to you ... perhaps even more so. The confidence which can be gained by learning to speak to a number of people at once is staggering. Through development of this art, your quest for success will be sharpened by the additional attributes *of learning to be in present time, adapting to any circumstances, responding in a pleasing manner to a variety of situations, articulating thoughts, pacing, leading, following, accepting your voice, standing upright, smiling, acting, and projecting a number of different emotions.*

I hope you agree that this subject is worthy of your attention.

In a reputable survey, when a large sample of the population in the United States were asked what they feared most ... public speaking was feared more than death itself. This is a staggering fact. Eminent scientists, prominent philosophers, great teachers and creative masters are all prone to this nuance of aberration. Why? *There is no hiding place,* is the answer that springs to my mind. When speaking in public, you bare all and take the consequences ... unless you are play acting or suffering identity substitution ... and even so you are still available for scrutiny to a greater or lesser degree.

Most of the greatest examples of humanity have been superb orators. This excellence is measured in many different ways of which you should be cognisant. As I have already mentioned, you may be thought of as a terrific communicator because of your ability to sit and listen. You may be liked because of the subject matter you embrace. Your excellence may lie in the tones of your instrument ... the vocal chords are as distinctive as fingerprints and so much more beautiful to scrutinize. Your physical appearance may be your major advantage, or perhaps it will be an ability to verbally project a feeling from within.

Whatever your main advantage may be, a few basic rules exist, that if followed will portray you in advantageous light, and at times may also extricate you from any tricky or uncomfortable situations that we all must confront at some times in our lives. I divide these guides on public speaking into colours and hope that these associations will help you at times when your attention will be most needed elsewhere.

The yellow guide states that you may never break an engagement once made. It is wise therefore, to be exceedingly careful before agreeing to speak, perform, teach or heal ... anywhere! The size or quality of the event is irrelevant within the teachings of this guide, which merely points out to you the fact that any negative judgement *of* you will cause an effect *on* you.

The blue guide makes the point that it is wise to have a space in which you may retreat and cause delineation between public performance and rest interval. You will realise the value of this the very first time you need to relax in order to maintain maximum power, yet some enthusiastic attendee wishes you to carry on with personal tuition, or whatever may be relevant to your given situation.

The red guide tackles performance. Unless you are playing King Rat in the pantomime Dick Whittington, I advise you in the first instance to *get the audience yes minded*, to use an old Dale Carnegie ploy. This approach encourages a degree of harmony from the outset, and you will make it more difficult for any group negativity to manifest. *Negaholics* can appear at a great variety of events, and the cleverest of them disguise their membership of *the negative attitude club*, or, the *NAC*, in intellect. By picking certain general *yesisms*, such as, *are we all agreed that ... wasn't that item in the news incredible* ... or you can even be blatant and humourous ... *1+1=2 correct?*, such tactics can make heckling harder to successfully accomplish by cleaving the rogue's tongue to the roof of its mouth. Yes minded tactics are psychologically based and absolutely permissible in the white hands of the honourable dabbler in PAC Magic.

The green guide asks if your topic is environmentally friendly, politically correct or revolutionary. Check the substance of what your talk is to be and compare it to the potential within the audience. Preaching a sermon on the advantages of ascetism, to a

114

group who are freshly into the starry world of personal development, will be less effective than a lecture with the same title as my first personal development book, *You Can Always Get What You Want.*

The black and white guide teaches you the relevance of dressing correctly for the occasion. It isn't clever to blatantly shock by such down scale tactics as choice of clothes. If the event calls for black suite and white tie then so be it ... you may utilise other means if your purpose is to shock, but be warned, your shocking tactics will rebound back onto you in the presence of a relatively pure audience.

The grey guide ... don't be boring ... be brief! Remember that *speeches measured by the minute, often die by the minute.* If you are worried about an audience's duplication of your material, or if the press have attended in force, be aware that *silence is the only part of your speech audible that they cannot ever misquote!*

The phantasmagorical guide teaches clarity of speech. By all means steer your audience into the mystical realms of interpretation, where no distinct lines may be challenged, but be lucid about your intent. Articulate in an acceptable fashion, and ensure that your accent does not lead an audience into preconception as to your intellect.

In my days of acting for a living, I was once told by an agents assistant, that when she suggested to him, an old theatrical type, that I should be put forward for the part of a photographer in a commercial, he replied in the negative ... *the chap has an accent!* She argued and won, I got the part and the script arrived for me to learn my lines, or line ... one line actually... *hold it; lovely!* Accent? ... I could have delivered it in any known earthly language including Sanskrit. Preconception must be understood and honourably manipulated, as this example illustrates.

The magenta guide instructs ... *keep your habits to yourself!*
Be pleasant and restrain all affectations. Twitches, coughs, nose
scratching and repetitive rhetoric will handicap you. Be warned
and stay clear. You may find that dedicated periods of TTM will
help you *still yourself,* thus eradicating useless mannerisms.

A London PAC Practitioner told me that he had spoken at
Speakers Corner in Hyde Park, London, the previous weekend to
our conversation. For those of you unfamiliar with this peculiarly
British phenomenon, it is located within a public London park,
where one may freely speak about anything to anyone at anytime.
Professional hecklers abound, rejoice and revel in their subversive
freedom; in so doing they provide invaluable practical guidance to
those of us wishing to excel in the honourable and ancient art of
public speaking.

Long live the hecklers!

Although a *baptism of fire,* he confessed it had taught him so
many lessons in such a short period of time, that he recommended
the endurance test to all PAC People, *as do I.* The practical
exercise which I shall now describe, is inspired by Speakers Corner
and all who frequent the place. I have formulated the following
simple procedure with fun in mind; if practiced, its mastery will
shield you from any barbed, verbal attack, and familiarise you with
many types of verbal discourse

✝

In similar fashion to the preceding exercise ... sit opposite a
partner, each holding any type of book or magazine from
which you will both alternatively read. The first person will
deliver one sentence from the publication. After it has been
delivered and understood, following a relevant and polite
but brief communication gap, a random insult should be
issued by the recipient. The type of antagonism utilised,

116

will depend on the category of communication in question
... *rubbish ... I disagree ... how do you know? ... cobblers ...*
phlegm sounds from the throat ... a shake of the head ... a
snarl ... a showing of the isolated middle finger ... along
with all swear words and a variety of deeply personal
insults, are all to be expected. Do not forget *to forget* the *no*
value judgement rule, even if you agree with what has been
said.   Yet again, alternate as presenter and recipient,
between you both. Persevere with this routine and you will
soon get used to accepting and delivering any type of
communication without ever being waylaid. I need not
remind you to leave the verbal contents of this exercise
behind you both, once an element of mastery has been
added to your repertoire. Always stop on a high, and
preferably when one or both of you have just cognited on a
communication area previously cloudy.

May I remind you that mastery of public speaking has more
relevance to general areas along a path stretching out before you
and culminating in an ever retreating boundary we classify as
personal success, than it has in talking to groups of people. *Trust*
me; try it and discover for yourself a short cut to super confidence.

Others and others
Let them get on with it, is a phrase frequently associated as an
observation of communication trends between people not directly
affecting you.   Communication between others does have a
personal effect however, and as such we need to embrace the idea
that mastery over our emotions connected with such external
dialogue and monologue, will aid our quest.

To begin with, I must point out that it is most beneficial to
understand that absolutely everything is endowed with an amount
of *consciousness*. The quantity, is in direct proportion to position
along the evolutionary line, and purity of soul. The densest portion

of a rock has consciousness, although, much as it is difficult for us human beings to contemplate the super human aspects of those who have transcended our present evolutionary state, so is it mentally demanding for us to consider the actual type of consciousness present in say, a pebble on the beach.

I am not theoretically imbuing non sentient matter with an intelligence which does not exist. Every single atom in physical reality is involved with its own process. Because an individual does not understand how to make a nuclear bomb does not lessen its effectiveness when exploded. I know enough about the atomic and spiritual aspects of nature to understand that it can only be the way I have described. If you are uncomfortable with this hypothesis then I urge you to take your studies further in order to satisfy your curiosity. Occult material is particularly suitable for this subject of consciousness, and I point you in that direction. As your psychic development proceeds, so will your faculty to assimilate previously absurd postulations.

The advantage of introducing you to *ubiquitous consciousness* in this fashion, is that anything even remotely approaching life potential, will now be easier for you to accept as an entity with individual qualities.

The cells which comprise your body is the subject matter which I feel needs to be illuminated if you are to reach the majority of benefits available from this subject of communication. You have 63 trillion cells at your disposal, each one a life within itself, and each one generating a small amount of energy. Every cell has a consciousness of its own. No matter how infinitesimally small an amount of will power each has, when combined into an organ, this power is multiplied accordingly. When you are healthy, the cells and organs of your body will be in harmony with one another to a greater extent; when you are poorly, that harmony will be to a lesser extent.

118

If you feel that organs do not have any inherent power ... what happens when one ceases to function? ... if the heart stops for long enough it will have exerted enough power to prevent useful accessibility to a physical vehicle by an all powerful spiritual being. Such power leads me to explore more possibilities even further!

The small amount of energy within each cell, multiplied 63 trillion times, becomes a force to be respected. It can work in your favour, or against your well being. It also demands of us an obligation to include *ubiquitous consciousness* within any equation medically calculated to preserve life. Of course the mainstream profession will only begin to do this when the possibilities of being laughed at have disappeared. Like everything throughout history, new concepts are first dreamed by the artistes of any culture ... or postulated by the *cultural-spiritual hierarchy!*

This however is not a new concept. The Tao is a grouping together of various aspects of ancient, Chinese mystical thought. There is no relevant Western equivalent; my thoughts on this subject are interpretations from this work, blended with spiritual theory from the Occult, and mixed vigourously into my forty one years of modern day living. We talk freely about communication, yet limit this pastime in the main, to social intercourse between similar beings. I feel that we should spend more time communicating with our organs, and developing a rapport with each of them. This way we will, as with everything, develop more affinity with them, as the quantity and quality of that communication rises. The beauty of this premise, is that one may develop such communication within any boundaries which feel comfortable to the individual.

Simple and general affirmations will suffice for many people ... *I have a healthy body ... I am the ideal weight for my height ... I love my body.* For the advanced PAC student, a more specific

119

approach may be tolerated ... *I have a healthy heart; its veins and arteries are clean; its physical health empowers it with a more loving outflow ... my fingers are agile and skillful; I perform many intricate tasks with them; their health empowers my creativity.*

A PAC Practitioner utilises any relevant technology that is available, in a quest for interdependent success. Advanced PAC Practitioners meditate deeply, and communicate with each of the interdependent organs that comprise their particular body. Cognisant of the *microcosm of the macrocosm theory,* they see the organs in their body as perhaps the planetary logos of earth sees us. In what type of manner does the planetary logos perceive the solar logos? What does the solar logos consider to be God? The One in whose Being we all live and breathe, is to us, what we are to our organs.

God!

We are all God! You can communicate directly with God as a culmination of inner exploration, for it is here that God dwells. Likewise, utilising the Hermetic axiom, *as above so below; as below so above,* you may communicate with your organs, and to a greater or lesser degree, control their efficiency. I understand that this may take some time to assimilate as a working tool of your chosen progressive route, but urge you I must to consider the advantages of this philosophy. In order to do this I suggest that you

✎

make a list of potential advantages connected to learning the art of inner organic communication.

A smile is the most powerful energy of personal power.

I encourage you to develop interdependent rapport between your organs through a sanction of smile. A true inner smile from your organs, will further encourage all other organs to contribute their power and make it available to the senses ... most especially the eyes. These two windows to the world are connected to all of your organs and senses. When you relax with a smile into calmness, you are able to maintain energy at a higher level than you would be otherwise capable of. This energy is immediately available for *action,* which is *the* key word in the positive lexicon at the vanguard of every Advanced PAC Practitioner's thoughts. The more energy you have, the more is available for improvement of personal skills. *As above so below* ... this data is equally relevant to both the facial smile, and the inner organ smile. How can you practise the inner smile? Are you brave enough to talk with your toe? Can you flow love and goodwill to a finger and accept its idiosyncrasies unconditionally?

人

TTM is the starting point of a process that will lead you into a deep meditation, which will allow intimate exploration of your inner world. Your attention can be focused on the astral plane, the mental plane or higher; just as it can be channelled towards a perception of your physical inside. If your body is healthy, then a general focus will invigorate it into a more enlightened service of you. If you have a particular problem with a specific organ ... the liver for instance ... then you must encourage it into positive service. Begin with a meditative smile directed towards the organ. Allow a return flow of information and mentally note intuitively, the potential cause of disharmony which is present in every single aspect of *dis-ease.* Stay in rapport until a smile is forthcoming from the relevant organ, and it is feeling more *at-ease.* You may return to this exercise as often as needed until the inner organic smile is of buddhic proportions. If you are able to accomplish this, you will find that good health will be in direct proportion to the amount of inner harmony you are able to perpetuate. As you master this occult type of inner communication, have your organs smile at one another in increasing quantities. The inner smile manifests also in an outward fashion.

Handling the others to others aspect of communication firstly from the extremely abstract angle of *the inner smile,* will now permit you a far easier transition towards the more external consideration of other people to other people, which I shall now call the Third Parties Facet or TPF. Especially in children, TPF forms a constant addition to their growing modus operandi ... they learn how to talk with others by referring to mental pictures of how their parents would do it ... they are frightened by violent interchanges between others ... they are moulded by chance acquaintance with the words of others to others.

We must be wary of this and naturally I support the notion of setting a good example. I also urge a mental domination over all that is heard as a TPF by you, the adult. Stay true to your own identity and do not ever be tempted to ID substitute for a personality that appears to be one towards which you aspire ... this is most obviously tempting when observing the TPF. It is also wise to avoid naming a child after any prominent member of the family ... this type of association frequently causes identity problems in early, if not the entire life of an individual.

Do not feel a constant need to interfere in the conversations or social intercourses of others ... grant the right for dialogue between others to occur without your participation, and adapt towards being merely a listener. If certain TPF becomes inflamed, then you may utilise your knowledge of the inner smile and transmit this flow towards the people in difficulty. It is a well accepted fact that *flowing love,* is the most altruistic remedy constantly available to each and every one of us. It is most efficacious when transmitted anonymously, a fact of which any Silent Knight is totally cognisant. It can be accomplished in many different ways ... *a pink beam ... a heart shape ... an auric pulse ... an abstraction of your understanding* ... choose your method and get into action when needed!

Power communication

An all knowing command of every aspect of communication is an obvious aspiration ... power communication will arrive in your life just as soon as you begin mastering each and every small aspect of the greater whole. TTM is the beginnings of your abilities to meditate deeply ... an activity which will take you into your inner space where the answers to every potential question you may have are readily available and easily accessible. God ... you the God ... the other God ... all aspects of God are available through your inner communications.

The universal mind is available to those of us willing to hone the art of inner exploration. There are many different grades of ether pervading each and every facet of life. One of the finest grades, is an ether which intermingles with everything you do, see, touch, perceive in any way, think or express. The slightest and faintest of thoughts will make an impression on this ether, and I have expressed this phenomenon as the Ether Waves in previous work, a descriptive phrase which I shall continue to use. Sometimes called the Akashic Records, Nature's Memory, The Book of God's Remembrance, amongst many others; this medium was utilised by Levi H Dowling in order to write his very excellent work called *The Aquarian Gospel of Jesus the Christ,* from which I have already quoted. It took him forty years of study and meditation to attain a level of spiritual consciousness necessary to attune to the distinct tones and rhythms left behind by *Jesus of Nazareth and the overshadowing Christ.* He considered the Ether Waves as sensitive plates on which sounds and thoughts were recorded on this, the finest of ethers.

These waves of lightform, were accepted by the Chinese from

123

ancient times onwards, within the concept of *Ch'i,* which is described as cosmic breath, and, a ubiquitous substance. The Hindus have the word *Prana* which describes a similar concept also. Unfortunately, much as the Eskimos necessarily have a large amount of words to describe a variety of snows, we do not have any word to describe what is called Ch'i by the Chinese and Prana by the Hindus, because we have not, up until recently, embraced the existence of this phenomenon I call the Ether Waves.

Franz Anton Mesmer, who was the originator of *mesmerism,* which led to the development of *therapeutic hypnotism,* also postulated the existence of an all pervading force which linked humanity together. In the second of his *Propositions Asserted,* he stated:

> *A universally distributed fluid, so continuous as to admit no vacuums anywhere, rarefied beyond all comparison, and by nature able to receive, propagate and communicate all motion ... this is the medium of the influence.*

It does not take that long for this universal mind to be reached in a general capacity. I utilised this facility very specifically earlier in this book, when I was unable in the first instance, to create a useful enough definition of the concept described by the word *morals* in guide three. I sought to differentiate between the very similar ideas of *ethics* and *morals;* I therefore lay on my bed and closed my eyes ... I was already tuned to a wavelength that is most beneficial to me whilst writing; it therefore happened very quickly ... a large billboard appeared, which I recognised as being at the top of Tanners Bank in North Shields; I had frequently read religious slogans on that same board when I was a child ... the picture faded a little after recognition, but I noticed that superimposed in a very abstract way, on the bottom of what seemed to be an otherwise unrelated advertisement, were the words ... *to be in tune with your conscience!* I smiled knowingly with inner contentment, and descended the stairs to work with these words, which provided us with a useful portion of guide three.

Do not for one moment think this a momentous occurrence, or in fact, that it is unique in any way. Most people tune in without knowing exactly what it is they are doing. In my earlier song writing days, I was under the impression that everything I wrote was totally and utterly original, as I sat with my guitar, a pencil and some paper and conceived. Maybe we need a fresh definition of the word original, because it is now my impression after working with the Ether Waves, that the sum total of everything capable of conception, is floating around on this substance ... we merely pluck from the universal store, that which we wish to utilise, and mould it in our own image. Now that this fact is known to me, I cooperate with the phenomenon, and by so doing, remain in harmony with an element of existence that abounds for the benefit of all.

Power communication begins with an acknowledgement of the Ether Waves. The concept is validated after your first successful tuning in to this universal mind. It is fulfilling when utilised in an unselfish manner ... this is a proviso for continued access. When passage is constantly sought amongst the Ether Waves for less than scrupulous ends, sooner than later, you will begin to deny yourself this inherent right of the philanthropist. Such denial may take any form suitable to successful restriction ... you may begin to repudiate the existence of such a phenomenon ... you may not succeed in manifesting anything worthwhile.

As all answers are within you, so are all obstacles.

It's all in the mind is the simple aphorism which manifests in my thoughts. This concept is found in all true success literature from Alice Bailey, who wrote of the concept with the words *energy follows thought;* to Napoleon Hill, who wrote about Cosmic Habit Force and coined the immortal phrase from the 1930's, *what the mind of man can conceive and believe, the mind of man can achieve.*

Those of you who have read the book, *You Can Always Get What You Want,* will be aware of my quest to discover a suitable source which modern day success literature could be attributed to. Napoleon Hill held some fascination for me because of his humble beginnings, which somehow led him into circles inhabited by a number of the richest and most famous members of the earlier twentieth century. There, was a man who was an excellent orator, equally at home with regular salesmen and high minded philosophers.

I knew that his source of inspiration had to be spiritual, because of the words he utilised in his writings. It was not until quite by chance, I was reading a biography called *The Real H P Blavatsky* by W Kingsland; it was noted that Thomas A Edison joined the Theosophical Society on the 5th of April 1878. I surmised it was through Edison, that Hill was introduced to the concept of cosmic consciousness at the beginning of the twentieth century, after they had become good friends. Although his work always had its *feet on the ground* so to speak, there were all those little tell tale give away signs that pointed towards his cognisance of higher teachings. Cosmic sources became apparent on studying his success formulae.

ϯ

Ask yourself a realistic question, the answer to which should not be in your memory. It must be within your general operating boundaries however, and you should firstly attain a *state of faith* in the workings of cosmic memory.
Faith is an absolute prerequisite to all aspects of pushing beyond normal limits ... I remember the very first radio interview I took part in after publication of my first book ...

the presenter asked cynically, "so Phil Murray, you're telling us that *You Can Always Get What You Want;* do you think I could become a brain surgeon?" I replied with the question, "do you think you could become a brain surgeon?" He said, "no!" I concluded, "then neither do I!"

I advise you to steer clear of irrelevant fact to begin with, and satisfy yourself with conceptual information, much as I have just described as being attained by myself for inclusion in guide three. Close your eyes and see the answer ... there is no time delineation relevant to this occurrence, as it is dependent on your own abilities and determination to improve them. Practice leads to mastery!

SK

Phil, as you know, you saw your answer, whereas another might hear it, feel it, even smell it? I mention this as a brief reference to those who have taken your reference to sight, literally.
... *end of note*

Telepathy is now a key word in the world of Personal Development. Most mainstream writers and teachers are embracing the concept, and to the degree that more people think about it and demand access to such wavelengths, is in exact proportion to the time scale allowing the phenomenon to become a regular occurrence in most peoples lives, much as television is to us now.

It is widely reported, or foretold, that telepathy will be an Aquarian attribute more readily made available to us for this new age, much as the steam engine heralded a dawning of the Industrial Revolution. An increasing number of people will also become aware of the much discussed fourth dimension; this will amount to increased perception of the etheric world, including the astral and mental planes.

The sum total of everything ever thought is recorded in the Akashic Records as I have already mentioned ... the exercise which followed encouraged a tuning of yourself into wavelengths containing reasonably specific data ... well, telepathy is not conceptually dissimilar. It is a subject which is ready to be written about by a competent author from the occult world, who is cognisant of the need for a readable and practical volume which the everyday reader can understand. This person should be capable of writing instructively and without jargon and incomprehensible phrases ... a complete book of this description should give us an accurate enough body of data to enable a discussion of the nuances relevant to all aspects of telepathy that we are currently able to contemplate.

The pineal gland, often erroneously referred to as the atrophying third eye, is a small organ in the brain, located between the eyes, the function of which is unknown to the mainstream medical profession. It is however, an evolving gland, and in fact, the instrument we have at our disposal which allows us to operate telepathically, so I believe. Some ideologies accord it the title, *seat of the soul,* and this it may very well be also.

It is helpful to become aware of this gland, and when communicating telepathically, to concentrate the thought you wish to transmit, whilst perhaps, becoming sensitive to a slight quivering feeling around this organ, which will in fact be a disturbance to the ether which surrounds it. It is the transmission of this vibration which will allow your thought to be received by another. *The transmission is active and the reception is passive.* Quite naturally, the power of your transmission will relate to your concentration ability in connection with the thought you wish relayed. Feeble thought will result in disappointment. Strong contemplation is an art which should be practiced, and when sufficient ability is evident, it is then that you should begin constructive use of telepathy. Practice will lead to perfection of technique, and render you a powerful force within the community of earth.

○

Ponder the amount of times so called co-incidences occur in your life ... *you are thinking about someone and they call you ... a letter arrives from a friend you have not seen in a long time, yet you were thinking about them at approximately the time when the letter was written ... your partner answers a question that was in your thoughts, yet you had not verbalised it ... you have an idea and discover that a colleague has the same one ...*

🏃

Deliberately and discreetly begin telepathically tuning in to the thoughts which surround you. As I have mentioned, *tuning* in is a passive activity; you need only become sensitive to the thought waves. Get the idea of being a *mental radio*. Begin this venture utilising your receiver initially. **Do not ever invalidate any feelings, perceptions or thoughts that may float your way** ... remember, the thoughts are there and you are merely practicing a dormant skill which others have already proved to be a latent power at the disposal of humanity. Be prepared for the less pleasant aspects of transmissions, and understand that it could be equally unpleasant for someone else if you likewise transmit lower impulses, telepathically. Once you decide definitely, that telepathy is part of your life, this is the time when it will become an increasingly real attribute within your universe.

Let me share with you a story which may add credibility to the claim that more and more of us are extolling the virtues of thought power, telepathy and the importance of right thinking. Because the idea began in the early part of the twentieth century, it also lends historical credence to the assertions ...

The Silent Minute

... quoted from *Writing on the Ground*, by Wellesley Tudor Pole ...

The idea began in 1917 when two British officers were discussing the war and its probable aftermath.

The conversation took place in a billet on the hillside at the mouth of a cave in the Palestine hills, and on the eve of a battle. One of the two, a man of unusual character and vision, realising intuitively that his days on earth were to be shortened, told his friend, who was Wellesley Tudor Pole: "I shan't come through this struggle and, like millions of others, it will be my destiny to go on. You will survive and live to see a greater and more vital conflict fought out in every continent and ocean and in the air. When that time comes, remember us. We shall long to play our part. Give us the opportunity to do so, for that war will be a righteous war. We shall not then fight with material weapons, but we will be able to help you if you will let us. We shall be an unseen but mighty army. You will still have "time" as your servant. Lend us a moment of it each day and through your silence give us our opportunity. The power of silence is greater than you know. When those tragic days arrive do not forget us."

Next day the speaker was killed. W.T.P. was severely wounded and left with the enemy, but managed to get back to the British lines with an inescapable sense of miraculous deliverance.

The idea of the Silent Minute was thus born in Palestine in December 1917. It came to external realisation in the dark days of Dunkirk twenty three years later when Britain stood alone and unprotected against overwhelming forces of evil. Men and women of goodwill in England and throughout the Commonwealth and elsewhere were then asked to devote one minute of their time at nine each evening to a prayer for peace, and thus to create a channel between the visible and invisible worlds. The movement grew until unknown numbers were united in keeping this evening tryst. This dedicated Minute received the support of H.M. King George VI, Mr Winston Churchill, his Cabinet and many other leaders in Church and State. The value was fully realised by the late President Roosevelt and by our Allies from overseas. The Minute was observed on land, air and sea, on the battlefields, in air raid shelters, hospitals and prison camps and in the homes of poor and rich alike.

At T.P.'s request and with the Prime Minister's support, the B.B.C. restored the voice of Big Ben to the air on Remembrance Sunday, November 10th, 1940, as a signal for the Silent Minute at nine each evening; and this became accepted practice in the Home and Overseas Service for the remainder of the war years and for some time afterwards.

According to the B.B.C. the number of those observing it in Britain and Europe from 1942 onwards ran into many millions.

Soon after the end of hostilities in Europe in 1945 a British Intelligence officer, interrogating high Nazi officials, asked one of then why he thought Germany had lost the war. This was the reply:

"During the war you had a secret weapon for which we could find no counter- measure and which we did not understand, but it was very powerful. It was associated with the striking of Big Ben each evening. I believe you called it The Silent Minute."
... *end of quote.*

This concept is now being re-instated ... as 10.00pm strikes, each evening, tens of thousands of people join together in thought, with a theme of peace and goodwill amongst humanity. Those who utilise the medium of prayer, may like to join forces with this thought and say ...

We pray thee, O God, to bring peace and goodwill amongst men.

A meditation can contain the sentiment as a seed thought ... all positive thought is both welcome and effective ... *you are invited!*

The whole spectrum of creation is the mental product of our pooled thoughts. Absolutely everything can be affected by thought impulses, and it is our duty to control the lower instincts which are present in all of us ... to a greater or lesser extent, and in various forms.

Power Communication includes an ability to restrain non creative thought impulses. This type of contemplation litters the astral world of desire, and clouds the planet's aura, thus obstructing a very beneficial ray of energy which is quickly becoming available to us. I will write more about energy rays in the following guide number five, called Happiness. Power Communication, as well as the esoteric aspects which I have described, is also about presenting yourself in the best possible light, without deception. You will be familiar with commercials on television which describe a product in a wonderfully tempting manner ... you buy the product and realise the advertising image was not part of the package. You must ensure that you do not short change those around you in this fashion.

Articulation is a visible indication of what is occurring within your mind. Learn the art and practice it. Speak clearly, describe creatively, and communicate precisely. In order to do these things efficiently, your thoughts must be in order, so that you may operate with a clear mind. TTM is the method whereby you may instantly achieve mental supremacy over your mind world ... govern the mental energy ... reign over your inner space ... control your internal time ... and subjugate all manifesting mind matter. You can do this! Those of you who persist with this goal in mind, will find after a short amount of time that this power communication has led you to a state where you, the spiritual being, have attained the state of *Cause,* over the vast mental world which you supervise and may rightly call your own.

Be proud of it!

Advanced PAC Practitioners are ... but what about happiness?

happiness

Guide Five

Serene, I fold my hands and wait,
Nor care for wind, or tide, or sea;
I rave no more 'gainst Time or Fate,
For lo! my own shall come to me ... *John Burroughs*

Where is it?

Happiness arrives during the accomplishment of an otherwise unrelated goal, is how I described the achievement of this most desirable abstraction in my first personal development book. I study and research with vigour, but I have yet to discover a more apt description of happiness. Its potential is everywhere, yet few of us, I venture to speculate, ever really tap into this mainly quiescent possibility with positive consequence.

In order to reach agreement on my definition of the word, I advise you to reflect over times gone by when you have been actively engaged in a pastime not related in any way to anything that you wished to do with your life. These periods rarely if ever result in happiness. Then reflect on your leisure activities, which are in themselves an important angle to be considered in this guide, usualy harbouring many goals and aspirations. Lastly think about overcoming obstacles en route to success and the feeling such accomplishment would give you.

Most people get tied up in social agreements on what has been agreed to be right and wrong ... *its wrong for a married man to leave his job to pursue an insecure goal ... a young man should go to university ... women are not good at manual work ... good people go to church ... if you have a job keep it ... you are playing when you should be working.* These are all examples of should's and should not's ... ought to's and ought not to's. Us Human Beings often allow a good proportion of our existence to be directed by

135

such clichés. They are however, a suppression of creativity!

The first rule for happiness is that there are no set rules; there are however guidelines. If these tips are married to whatever is inside you ... they can help set you on course for a human consideration of serenity. I advise you in the first instance, as with everything you wish to accomplish ... **decide that it is already in existence!**

Smile with the simple repetitive affirmation which follows, and this commitment will get you into action in a beneficial direction ... *I am happy!*

Say it in a variety of fashions; laugh as you repeat it; get serious and shout it; stick your tongue out after saying it; then ring someone up, the closest person to you this lifetime, and tell them all about it. Make a commitment with this person and yourself, to happiness.

It was mentioned at a PAC Gathering, that stating something which is not as yet true, is tantamount to lying. My answer to this is simply that everything is exactly as you say it is in your *Perfect World of Mind,* as Henry Thomas Hamblin calls it in his excellent book *Dynamic Thought,* and it is only a question of time before the physical universe will accept your truthful mental concept, as physical fact.

I am happy!

Stating this fact has now settled you into a commitment which will only last while your are on course towards actual accomplishment. In order to maintain momentum you must immediately set the wheels of the physical universe in motion, by conceiving and then writing down, your thoughts in connection with *your mission in life!* This word mission probably has religious beginnings and connotations, but these possibilities are irrelevant unless stimulating to you. I want you to embrace what I call a *theosophically karmic attitude* to this exercise. The theosophical angle is the divine wisdom which states that we are here to work out our own destinies. The karmic angle I will treat superficially in this guide, as more time will be spent with the concept later in connection with achievement.

During the course of my various investigations I have come across many weird and wonderful concepts of history and the speculative subject of where we all came from. One area taught me that we were all expelled from another planet for being either artists, rapists or murderers ... I was relieved to be known as a songwriter during those studies. Another stated simply that we are matter, and when dead, we return to the earth ... no divine inspiration there. God created man in his own image ... that phrase hit home for me. Evolution? ... an incomplete study!

Between the subjects of Theosophy, Esotericism, Mysticism, the Occult, Rosicrucianism, Christianity, Buddhism, Hinduism ... *upward, onward et al* ... we find some interesting common threads. *He who knows but one religion, knows none,* states the ancient aphorism. It is through an understanding of our heritage that we will be more able to gird our loins in a quest for success, during which, happiness *will* be forthcoming.

I spent four years of my life subjectively studying my own history in the nature of this lifetime and past lives. I can safely vouch for the fact that past lives are easily reached through very simple procedures. The purpose for so doing here, is to give you a factual indication of the Divine Potential within us all. Some of you will already be aware of previous existence, just as others will need to spend an inordinate amount of time weeding through irrelevant episodes of their present era before the veil is cast aside.

As we do not have the purpose of handling any particular problem with this past life regression exercise which follows, I advise you to ...

instantly write down the first thing that comes into your head when asking yourself the question ... *what would I most like to achieve in this lifetime?*

Using TTM and this goal which you have just written down, ask yourself ... *is there an earlier time when I wished to achieve ...(whatever the goal is) ... when was that ... (write down the date without questioning its validity)*

Each time you receive an answer, write it down, and repeat the question again. You will reach a point when you may feel cynical about the response, as it could seem too abstract; or the date, either because you are tempted to question a this lifetime period, or, it is something like 91,321 years ago ... a span you are unused to dealing with.

Phil, I only inject this as additional information based on facts discussed even in the hallowed halls of so-called Scientific Methodology. You have just written about accessing the events list from a Being's past time track, during which many bodies will have been utilised. Human bodies also have a genetic past which can be accessed, and sometimes gets confused with the Being's own back track. Of course the genetic track will have been interwoven with the earthly existence of many different Beings.

It is a fact that no living cell has existence without having emerged from the division of another cell, and its character, or uniqueness, is derived from the *mother* cell, and this we call DNA. It may not be a fact that its *aura* or etheric double derives from and is the same as its *mother*. But why not? It is not too difficult to agree if we accept etheric doubles for a complete body of cells! Of course it is a fact that there is a mysterious *intelligence* at work accomplishing this marvelous chain of events, which has a *memory* of how it is done, and possibly all the trials and battles that it went through during the huge millennial time intervals that have passed during its life. This *memory* has been called a Time Track by some opinion, and Carl Jung calls it a Race Memory when he discusses Archetypes. It is thought possible that the Being is able to view two past time tracks ... his own and that of the body he utilises as a physical vehicle, which is governed by what is called a Genetic Character. The Being can thus become confused as to which collection of events he is viewing. If we ponder on this, we have right here in *this moment* trillions of cells that are actual *pieces* of the first cell of the first human of our genetic line! This is a *fact*. Partly cognisant of the intelligence behind all this, is it too farfetched to state that we have access to the memory banks of all the *bodies* that preceded this one we currently utilise? *This is not to be confused with what you have written about the Akashic Records and what you call the Ether Waves.* Think of it! Such contemplation can boggle the mind! During any past life regression exercise people must never debate whether or not we have lived before ... that discussion should occur before any such activity is instigated. If past lives are discounted as unfeasible by people, then it is well that such doubters nevertheless partake of the exercise and conclude that they are imagining what they are seeing ... and then imagine some more! Where is this imagination coming from so easily? Who should worry so long as such activities are enlightening and they help people become less aberrated. This fact-supported idea is often more palatable for many western minds.

... *end of note.*

We all have varying methods of thinking ... some in black and white, or coloured pictures ... some in audio mode only ... some in abstract forms ... some in symbols ... and it has to be said, some hardly think at all and rely on a kind of animalistic stimulus response operating basis to get by. None of the latter will be reading this book, but it is as well that you know the varying degrees of inner perception that exist.

You may wish to linger and peruse these pictures when they are offered up for your viewing pleasure by your *inner world secretary,* but I advise you to utilise this technique for its purpose, which is to gain proof of previous existence. If there is an uncomfortable amount of emotion in a given incident, you may feel a need to discontinue the process and return to it when you have regained composure. If you are currently taking medication of any description, then I advise you to wait until these chemicals are eliminated from your system before attempting past lives regression. Similarly, make sure that you have not drunk anything alcoholic within the previous twenty four hours as this can also have an adverse effect on your chances of success. Remember always that you are in command; this is your inner space, and the facilities to be found living therein are at your disposal. In this world you *are* God!

If the past life process is taking longer than you first anticipated, then you may wish to continue reading this book, and periodically return to the process until success is forthcoming. Enjoy the experience ... it should not be an endurance test.

We have all lived numerous times before and most of us will need to incarnate many more times again, before our processes will be complete. Some are more advanced than others, and it has been recorded for instance, that the spiritual being known as Christ, when living during Atlantean times, was one million years ahead of the then current evolutionary process. It is as well that such possibilities exist, as without the accelerated progress of some, I feel evolution would have suffered a set back, perhaps costing us millions of years longer enduring this physical process.

So, we are aware of some subjective history. We also have a

goal written down, which was the result of asking a specific question before the past lives process. I would like you now to work with this ambition and ...

○

Ponder the goal conceptually. Think about all aspects. Reflect on its various angles. Generally illuminate your future utilising the words which were offered to you by your inner world secretary.

It is rare for these instantaneous answers to be useless. It is common however, for people to be embarrassed about having goals which differ greatly from their present circumstances. You are en route to success, and you will need to be bigger than any thoughtform which surrounds you, that has become so strong through repetition, it now has an apparent beingness all of its own which has begun to work against you ... it is called *HABIT!*

Before you make a decision as to whether or not you will pursue the goal, continue with the technique which I am presenting to you. It may help your decision making procedure.

Using the subject of the goal, I want you to ...

✎

Compose into one succinct sentence, your complete aspiration, and call it a Mission Statement. Beneath it, compose a Visualisation Statement, as wild as you like, containing everything as you wish it to be. More complete examples of this process can be found in my first personal development book *You Can Always Get What You Want.*

The mission statement is a physical indication of what goes on inside your head. We are all involved in this world of cyclical phenomena; it must be understood that fashions and fads are transient, and not to be confused with the innate purpose of you the individual. Some readers will have hit the jackpot by locating the goal which is central and pivotal to their present existence on earth ... perhaps a goal at which they have been working for the last few lifetimes. Others will have cognited on lesser goals which are nevertheless important. The remainder will comprise of people too busy with side issues to spend time contacting the one aspiration which could prove the only route to happiness they will ever encounter.

This mission statement is not sacred ... you can play around with it and discover the best angle at which to approach this powerful tool. Skillful questioning of yourself is an aid which can accelerate the process of location. You can try *changing places!* This involves questioning yourself as a third party ... for me this would entail the following scenario as an example ... *what would Phil Murray wish to do with his life? What is the one thing on earth that Phil Murray would enjoy being involved with for the rest of his life? If anything was possible, what would Phil Murray choose as a profession?*

Sometimes it is better to ask yourself similar questions and leave your inner world secretary to provide you with answers ... which will usually be forthcoming within a seven day period or less. If you utilise this method, then you must be alert to the mental process which will provide you with answers. Write any potential solutions down on paper so that you may ponder them at leisure.

If you have the major purpose you wish to work with for this lifetime, then you may find it helpful to begin qualifying this direction with subsidiary questioning. For me, this would involve a process similar to the following example ... if Phil Murray could write about anything he wished, what would that subject be? ... if this person Phil Murray was unable to write, what then would he do? ... if Phil Murray had three million pounds in cash, would he still write? This last question of a particularly helpful type as it focusses a person on individual purpose in an indirect way.

Sometimes, the visualisation statement, which is the wild and less controlled aspect of this mission technology, can stimulate your imagination into a more accurate composition of your succinct, one sentence mission statement. Play with the ideas and discover what works best for you ... not being an automaton means that all generic types of personal development data must be either customised by the individual, or more expensively it can be done for you with personal consultations. I advise you to do it yourself ... such tactics are always ultimately more fulfilling.

The Seven Beams from Outer Space, via the Milky Way
The sheer diversity of personalities involved in the game of life at any one time, is the only aspect of physical existence which makes human life tolerable ... *you may feel that it is only fellow mankind that is making your life a misery ... you can ask why people do not know better ... desperation can be exhibited at the shortcomings of your neighbours* ... but take away the rest of humanity and that would just leave you! Could you stand that idea as reality.

I am sure that in your Premier State of spirituality, *at-one-ness* would be enjoyable, as would at-one-ness between spirit, mind and body during incarnation. All of my intuition however, together with the main body of research in which I find myself engaged, tells me that, just as we were as one to begin with, so shall we be as one at the end of this cycle of constant reincarnation. I call this *Premier State*, and visualise it as the blissful *nothingness of togetherness*.

Yet again, through taking this ultimate postulate of Premier State as our ideal, we can see that it is as a group, our future is to be best enjoyed. Opinion on this axiom seems to be in agreement,

143

throughout all of the esoteric sources which I both utilise and respect. For the near future, the formation of groups seems to be of paramount importance to facilitate *the reappearance of The Christ*.

At the dawning of each new astrological age, an Avatar appears to impart relevant wisdom, aimed at an understanding of the particular qualities available to humanity, through the major energies prevalent for the following two thousand three hundred year period ... or thereabouts. Avatars also appear at any time when it is felt that there is a need for divine principles to be imparted to the masses as a guidance to humanity.

Hercules was an early example, who illustrated helpful principles in his *Twelve Labours of Hercules*. Hermes Trismegistus followed; the thrice great Hermes who proclaimed himself *Light of the World*. Vyasa was another, who taught that death was not the end ... Buddha gave us the *Four Noble Truths,* and prophesied the coming of Christ, whom he said would follow him. Shankaracharya was another, and Shri Krishna of the *Bhagavad Gita,* whom many people believe to have been a previous incarnation by Christ.

The Christ of two thousand years ago, taught love and forgiveness, which were new concepts to many, and the existence of the human soul. He lived a life of sanctity in incarnation and asked nothing for himself. He was the highest manifestation of spiritual qualities that could be achieved at that time. The fact that many of his teachings were taken out of context, leading many religious groups into a mere shadow of his true intentions, is a human failing, just as is our desire to seat an anthropomorphic God on The World Throne.

There are many different groups of people in quite separate existences, who believe that exactly what I have just described as *the reappearance of The Christ,* is imminent. We must remember that Christ The Being, is also a quality of love which exists in each of us. I believe that the actual word Christ, loosely means *The Anointed One.* The consensus of opinion is that the initial stage of this reappearance will be an overshadowing of suitable disciples with the Christ quality. As Head of *The Spiritual Hierarchy,* it is part of his duty to manifest when needed, but, just as any spirit crystallizes in the presence of matter, unless we raise the vibrations of the planet to a more hospitable level, this reappearance will be less beneficial than might otherwise be the case.

Djwhal Khul encouraged the formation of a *new group of world servers* in his writings through Alice Bailey, and some of the people which comprise this group, will be utilised for such purpose of overshadowing, along with *all* peoples of goodwill and service. Through this manner of awareness, the astral quality of desire will be raised enough to allow The Christ to live amongst us ... not necessarily in any religious capacity, but in the most beneficial manner possible to the world need. It is hoped that he will impart the seed wisdom which will allow maximum benefits for the evolutionary process during the Aquarian Age.

It was widely believed that when, nearer the beginning of the twentieth century, Bishop Leadbeater and Annie Besant adopted the person known as Krishnamurti, he was to be the one prepared for overshadowing by The Christ, as had occurred two thousand years prior with the Master Jesus. Although he led an extraordinary and spiritually influential life, he denied himself as an Avatar, and perhaps did not allow the process to occur.

Those of us who possess Christ Consciousness, prepare the way and spread the ideas of love, light and forgiveness wherever they will be accepted. Anyone can do this, and the work can take many forms. The Silent Knight philosophy is an example available through this book, of anonymously transferring thoughts of love

145

and forgiveness into the world ... this is Christ Consciousness, just as is the most fanatical manifestation by some, of the nail holes He suffered two thousand years ago, in their physical bodies.

This Christ Consciousness does not have to be a mystical process, in fact quite the contrary; spreading love, light and forgiveness can be as simple as holding your tongue, or smiling in the face of adversity. Whether you believe in such a reappearance or not, the spreading of love, light and forgiveness is surely to be preferred to their opposites of hatred, darkness and revenge!

Through example, Christ taught that happiness occurred during the following of spiritual impulse. Stepping this down a degree or more, this relates simply into the fact that if you seek happiness as a personality, the best you can expect is a transient thrill or a titillation of the senses. I would equate such aspiration with the accomplishment of a ride on a rollercoaster in a fairground. This type of personality happiness is frequently addressed by short sighted psychological counselling, as well as old fashioned and un-*spiritually*-educated personal development teachers.

You are spirit living in matter and both qualities place differing demands on an individual. I hazard the postulate that most of us would find a totally spiritual existence whilst incarnate, impossible ... and if it is possible, then totally uncomfortable were it to be achieved during a lifetime. You must serve the body, and treat it well. Keep it healthy and free from poisons. It is the temple in which you, the spirit, dwell. The more healthful your body is, will correspond to the degree in which you can live a spiritually fulfilling existence ... this is what will lead you to happiness!

You are also responsible for the progress of human bodies and their suitability for the incarnation of presently disincarnate souls. Blend the physical personality with the character of the soul ... if you can do this then you will be privileged. This cannot be accomplished through denial of any human aspect of life. You must embrace all possible blends in an effort to find the combination which suits. What I describe as *the seven beams from outer space, via the milky way,* are in fact seven well acknowledged energies with greatly differing qualities, flowing onto planet earth from a cosmic source, stepped down in intensity and redirected in the milky way, before finally arriving at their destination. They are more widely known as the *Seven Rays,* or *the Seven Rays of Energy* ... Plato called the phenomenon *Seven Spirits,* and another name for them is *Seven Lamps before the Throne of God.* Pick the one you like ... I think the *Seven Rays* will suffice, and my heading for this section of the book, although accurate, would perhaps be more fitting as the title for a movie, and is indicative of my background in entertainment.

Each of us is bound in the energies of one particular ray predominantly, and some of the remainder secondarily. Each aspect of the human combination will also illustrate a dominant quality; so you can see that the sooner a *Seven Ray Science* is developed, the quicker we will be capable of fully understanding our potential and limitations. Scientists acknowledge the existence of these energies, but without the occult key, they will be unable to progress with their concrete appraisals of the phenomena.

I write about this subject as a sub heading of the happiness guide, because a knowledge of the Rays will help you understand yourself, although I see little point in closely evaluating your existence utilising this new science without a much deeper understanding of it, which I am ill qualified to impart. Utilise the information available here in a general manner, and those of you wishing to progress further in this field should contact ...

The Lucis Trust, Suite 54, 3 Whitehall Court, London SW1A 2EF.

There is also a book called *The Seven Rays of Energy,* by Michal J Eastcott, which you may like to purchase directly from Sundial House, Nevill Court, Tunbridge Wells, Kent TN4 8NJ.

The Qualities present in the rays are as follows ...

The first ray is will and power; the second ray is love-wisdom; the third ray is active intelligence; the fourth ray is harmony through conflict; the fifth ray is concrete knowledge and science; the sixth ray is devotion and idealism; the seventh ray is order and ceremony.

These descriptions are of qualities and consciousness; for our knowledge of them, we are dependent totally on their manner of manifestation through us humans. We are able to exhibit these qualities to the degree that we have cleansed the physical vehicle. As we all possess both spiritual and material aspects, those of us still languishing in the depths of our outmoded animal instincts, will display exhibitions of lower harmonics; those of us who have transcended the lower facilities, will be more able to embrace a purer form of the descriptions so given.

Manifestations of these qualities are obvious ... the first ray may produce leaders who exert will and enjoy power; *ponder the higher and lower aspects of that description* ... the second ray predisposes people to a gentler side of human nature ... the third ray is apparent as busy, practical, efficient, intelligent and capable qualities are visible in a person's life ... the fourth ray has always seemed paradoxical to me, yet the more you reflect on it, the easier an understanding of it becomes; sensitivity and imagination alongside awareness and artistic temperament ... the fifth ray embraces the world of science; it is intellectually focussed in the mind and can be analytical and critical ... the sixth ray is obvious in fanatics and perfectionists ... the seventh ray can be seen in organised people who respect law and order.

The soul can be of a certain ray, and the body born into a different ray. Blending of the rays is infinite in variety and diverse as the universe itself. The rays themselves have other qualities less apparent in them, and the variations within both them, and the human duality, produce the wonder of life on planet earth. If you are able to pinpoint your soul ray then it could go a long way towards aligning a powerful mission statement and visualisation statement, into your life. I urge you not to get bound up in significance, and this can very easily become the case for many during the discovery of life's fundamentals.

The Occult is not black magic as is popularly believed, although such knowledge can be used in this way. Literally and practically, it is the science and study of energy. The word itself can also mean *hidden*. In astrology, an occultation of the moon is a Lunar Eclipse ... so the definition maybe should include something to do with *obscured*. I suggest that occult scientists should make available to us all, some practical work on the blending of this knowledge into our every day lives. It is certainly the next stage of study for Advanced PAC Practitioners who have spiritually transcended what their present studies can give them.

Happiness is knowing yourself and accepting whoever you are. It is not complacency. Do not excuse your participation in life because you are not that type of person. Every different variety of human has a role to play in the process of life on earth and true happiness is the living of that role which you know to be yours!

Find out what your goals are ... meditate on who you really are ... and if by now you have not separated yourself, the soul, from your vehicle, the body, then a simple exercise will help you on your way. I have read chapters in books on the kingly science of the soul, *Raja Yoga*, that describe this knowledge of the various human

149

aspects as being fundamental to spiritual progress. I agree, and I have yet to discover a simpler and more pragmatic exercise than the one which I use for the illustration and separation of you, the spirit.

↑

Utilising TTM, create a picture in your mind of a car. Colour this car red and give it a sporty appearance. Make the interior spacious and give the seats a thick covering of pink velour. Park the car on a gravel drive outside a mansion which incidentally belongs to you. Start the car and rev it up. Drive it along a deserted road at fast speed, then return it to your drive and park it up. Say goodbye to your creation, make it disappear and open your eyes.

○

Who made the picture ... *you made the picture* ... where was this picture ... *it was in your inner mental world of mind* ...

There is a simple rule in psychology which states that *you cannot be what you are looking at.* If you are looking directly at something, not its reflection, then you *must* be separate from it. Think about that for a while and ponder the implications. Utilising this rule, we can understand that you are not the body which you can see; nor are you the picture which you created. You are you! A spiritual being with the ability to achieve consciousness on earth through the mental world onto this physical plane.

SK

This may not be real to those unsure about *Out Of Body Experience,* yet, this subject which we can also call *Exteriorization With Full Perception,* is the ultimate goal of most self realization technology. Buddha was successful and was perhaps the first example of this state ... *clear of the body* ... but this is not an easy goal to attain by most people.
... end of note

You the spiritual being, innately have the ability to create, and perceive your creations.

In human form we utilise creation in mental matter, and such creation always precedes its physical counterpart. Working in mental matter is important to the age in which we live. Raja Yoga is the relevant exercise for our time period, as was Hatha Yoga in Lemurian times, for the development of an awareness of the physical body which was in its infancy, and ... Laya Yoga then Bhakti Yoga for the development of the etheric and astral bodies during Atlantean times.

The human being is in a period of mental evolution and consequently it is quite retrogressive to practice any of the yogas which were relevant in previous times, as the greater yoga always includes any benefits available from the lesser in results, although not necessarily in practice.

✎

A book for further reading on this subject is *Raja Yoga or Mental Development,* by Yogi Ramacharaka ... a Yogi publications book.

Of course, the separation of human aspects is not quite as simplistic as I have made it out to be. But this approach will help you along the path towards a fuller knowledge of the different worlds. Some of you will follow the mystical path of feeling, and some will travel the occult route of fact; but it is a blending of the heart and mind which will produce the most powerful results. If the modern alchemist follows my simple guidelines through the utilisation of PAC Principles, then an accelerated journey towards spiritual fulfillment, and the lesser emotion of happiness, will be forthcoming.

151

Forcing a smile

I have often stated that the Positive Attitude Club is not about smile training, and in saying that I was quite wrong. Of course, I meant it in the way big business is teaching employees to smile, which they then often do without really meaning it. This is an exercise dedicated to an increase in profits. Well, I should have known better, because I have often used the forced smile to evoke the real smile.

I must confess that I used to perform one night stands as an entertainer, and towards the latter part of that section of my history, resentment crept in and I began to develop an antagonistic attitude towards my audience. I would often remain backstage in a state of moroseness, until just before performance time, when I would jump up and down shouting *yes! yes! yes!* and look in the mirror, forcing a smile until I laughed. My spirits rose as did my energy level, and I was able to make an entrance looking like the professional which I am.

At the time I felt false about utilising this psychological trick, yet I now feel that it is admissible as an aid. Unless your condition is chronic, I see no reason why you should not force a smile to raise your spirits. It is worthwhile noting why you are feeling less than fully resourceful, but remember that we are human and subject to physical demands and limitations.

Smiling causes a physiological reaction in the human being, which automatically helps towards a mental focus on happiness, by releasing the *misery pull* from the body to the mind. If you are feeling down, as we all do at times, then try forcing a smile onto your face until it takes over and forces you into better spirits. The act of smiling is also an excellent facial exercise, as it uses many more muscles than frowning. Record an audio cassette tape programme of funny sayings ... spend some time collecting your favourites or glean them all in one fell swoop from library books of humour. Walking upright, with straight shoulders and a vertical back is also a subliminal signal to the body that happiness is a more relevant manifestation than misery. Deep breaths of fresh air help in a bodily way ... but like all of the lesser yogas I previously described, these tricks have been superseded by a need for the increased mental ability which can be brought about through practice of Raja Yoga ... this does not mean that you cannot transiently dip back into the past for a boost.

Forcing a smile is also a service to others. Do you prefer a smile or a frown on your colleagues. Please do not think for one moment I am condoning falseness. Forcing a smile is the physical manifestation of a mental decision ... the physical forcing angle is merely an acceleration of a process that would have to happen anyway under natural law. *Before the beginning is a thought, and the absolute purpose of that contemplation is creation,* is how I worded this natural law in my second personal development book. Every single physical creation that ever existed, began life as a thought ... I have no problem accelerating my mental decisions into physical manifestation, and I urge you to consider doing so ... providing as ever, your intentions are honourable.

There is also the forcing of a smile by the human who lives life in covertly hostile mode. This example of humanity usually brandishes a knife behind the back whilst so doing. I steer clear of such people as I find little to *like* in them, but I always flow love and forgiveness their way.

Joy

Whenever you criticise another, you pin a part of your beingness to that criticism and until you release it, you have wasted attention units destructively. You need all the attention units available to you in any quest for success, and PAC Practitioners cherish each and every one of them ... individually!

Phil, this concept of attention units is new to many, and although you have already discussed the subject earlier in the book, perhaps readers could use a little more explanation and clarification. I cannot remember my source, but a Master Teacher was once asked what one word was most important in gaining Nirvana, Self Realization or Rapid Development. His answer was ATTENTION. All life is vying for attention or trying to avoid it, depending; something is BIG, mentally, if important, and small conversely. Importance and importances are a not-so-recognized factor in the mastery of our attention ... **attention units are** *life givers* **to thought forms** ... this should help clarify your use of the phrase. We could both meditate on this as a subject in itself, I think, and get to the very mechanics of what you are successfully accomplishing with this subject you call EMPOWERMENT.

... end of note

Mental criticism is a problem that we will increasingly come to terms with in our psychological study of the inner world of mind. As with all activities, practice of *mental criticism denial,* will lead you to perfection in the art of so doing. Your mental world is available to anyone well versed in the science of telepathy, but numbers of such people, although increasing on a daily basis, are few and far between.

Oral or written criticism is more obvious, and can chain you to a given remark for a whole lifetime. Do you want this to happen? Think deeply and count three days before indulging in self destruction of this paradoxical nature. What gives you the right to criticise anyway? You can have likes and dislikes ... and make others aware of them. You can reprimand bad behaviour which is factually demonstrated as destructive and harmful ... but for your own good as well as any potential victim ... don't!

Joy and gladness are flavours that will pass your way in direct proportion to the amount of times they are invited into your life, monitored by the quality of your outflows. Yet again, what you put out will return like a boomerang, unfailingly. Joy and gladness are no exceptions.

It is often a shortcoming within an individual, to look at the life of a less than scrupulous colleague and announce an imbalance ... *he is always treading on peoples toes, yet look at that, the boss gives him a promotion! ... she treats men like dirt and they always come back for more ... my friend steals whatever he needs and he has all the things I want ... she lives a life of luxury and never has a kind word for anyone!* ... yet I guarantee you this, the balance *will* always exist. *How,* is often imponderable! If you want to invest in the church of your heaven, give joy in this lifetime and understand the universal law of return. Superficial judgement of surrounding colleagues will not ever show you their real insides ... the pain in the heart ... the black ice on their path ... the dark spot in the centre of their inner mental sanctum. Likewise, and this must be ever born in mind ... the service of an individual is not always visible and it is humanly tempting to criticise a person for what appears to be an apparent shortcoming. Do not risk this type of thought ... a Silent Knight can be anyone.

Goodwill

This seems to be a key word in the vocabulary of the *new group of world servers,* begun by the Master Djwhal Khul, yet I wonder just how much lip service this quality is given without active support. If you were able to *be* goodwill, then I venture to postulate that your life on this planet would not be necessary any longer, and you would be more able to choose a less painful existence elsewhere.

The truth is that few of us are able to maintain such a high soul quality as this surely is, whilst living a normal life of work, family, leisure and ambition. So, just like unconditional love which we discussed earlier, we must aspire towards ever more amounts of

155

this outflow we call goodwill. It can be more easily understood as a quality, by changing the terminology around a little to illustrate it as an action ... *the will to good!*

That means using your will power, which can be awesome when trained, and will good ... to, in, for, at, under, over, sideways and around whoever or whatever you like! It is interesting to note that whilst willing good, you cannot have critical thoughts. You can stop the goodwilling and retract it because that person did not deserve it, but I get the feeling you have transcended such sentiment, at the very least in theory.

⋏

Following a quick fix of forgiveness, which will be felt by you and the recipient, flow goodwill to that person as a solid, concentrated thought of relevant pleasantry. Note your relief. Go one step further and demonstrate this goodwill physically to them with an appropriate action. Various reactions to this can be expected and you must ready yourself for all eventualities, including rejection.

Whatever happens, the mental flow of goodwill must persist, as this is the *senior service* that you are performing! This universe is a mental creation, and we are at that part of our evolutionary process where we are able to partake of the powers available to us through use of the mental plane. This means that Karma will also be generated on this plane in ever increasing amounts for you ... both good and bad ... which do you want?

Laughter

The simple and most effective on the spot cure for any down period you may experience in your life is laughter. Chronic doses of it at an appropriate time will actually lift you into a higher mental compartment, thus making access to the depress causing stimulus impossible. Comedians are the best access to this fix, as they are external to the processes which started the depression.

My friend, a Silent Knight, has made up his own audio cassette tape programme, an idea which I also mentioned earlier, which he calls *chuckles, punnies and pithies* ... this is a collection of one liners and illustrates his belief in such therapy. *A little nonsense now and then, is relished by the wisest men,* states the old saying. I believe that wise men have contingency plans for those times when they need a quick lift from the blues. I have a number of humourous thoughts which I can call on in an emergency. I advise you to contemplate this issue in advance, for when it happens it is too late.

The path leading towards spiritual improvement and ultimate success, does, it should be noted, have its ups and downs. It is written in many places that one must take care when introducing someone to this vast and powerful body of knowledge, as it can be incredibly disruptive to an otherwise orderly, though non spiritually cognisant, life. It falls upon the Karma of the presenter when such introductions are premature. It is part of my role as *Leader of the PAC* to make such transitions available from the path of Personal Development to the Path of Spiritual Development, and I therefore gladly continue such service by medium of this book and its associated audio cassette tape programme.

Not all students or teachers of the ageless wisdom will be in agreement with what I have written here; not for its *content,* but for its *intent* ... the making available of hitherto hidden knowledge, to whomever feels ready for it. I say to such doubters, that times are changing as are the rules. This information no longer exists just for use by the chosen few. A sufficient quantity of earth s inhabitants are adequately advanced in the mental realms to take care of any premature accidents, and responsible enough to not abuse the knowledge ... *I hope-a-hope!*

Spiritual Development can get too serious in my opinion, and this subject of laughter is just the thing to remind us of our lighter aspects. *If it gets too serious,* I always say, *then ask why?* If it isn't fun *then it isn't the PAC!* Remember that true spiritual achievers, rarely if ever, advertise the fact. A friend of mine recently told me that she had been to see an Avatar for a consultation in Germany; yet I cannot imagine a person with such spiritual progress behind them advertising ... *Avatar available for consultation!* I don't deny the good such people do, but we should remember the *cry wolf* saying and hope that when the real thing arrives we are not too complacent to accept.

I invite you to laugh and keep laughing; frequently and fervently. Laughter is the *ability* to reject importances. Do not utilise it as a cover up, or a nervous shield, but as a measure of your true success and a reflection of your inner happiness. Help other people laugh too ... it is contagious ... as is ...

The contagion of serenity
This state of serenity is an *of the sky* experience of placidity and tranquility, in a place of quiet solitude, whilst amongst others.

That is my definition and I use it to describe a potent feeling of inner knowingness. It is an aspiration of worth and even its lower harmonics are contagious. Needless to say that those people manifesting the real thing, attract anybody and everybody. You therefore need to be able to hold your space in such busy situations, thus further proving that this true state breathes and lives within you.

We must understand that repressive people exist, whose sole purpose is to undermine achievement. The cleverest of them all appears nothing like you would expect and is probably even in a position of power and influence. Repressives are particularly attracted and susceptible to the contagion of serenity, as they are totally unable to generate even the lower harmonics by themselves. Nor do they want to. As they cannot conceive of this aspiration mentally, they will never be able to experience it physically.

Repressives content themselves with the destruction of others, and if they existed in the world of occult magic, then you could call them black magicians. Thankfully, few such people exist, and we should therefore, not waste attention units on them. Repressives however, are to be kept at arms length, and if possible, avoided altogether. You need to be in a position of mental power to maintain your prowess in their presence, as they will continuously seek methods with which to covertly undermine your beingness.

The much maligned and misunderstood word, *Occult,* simply means the *science or study of energy,* as I have already said. It has been frequently misused to describe black magic, and has now almost become synonymous with the dark, left hand path. It is a word which will come into its own in the coming years, as the ageless wisdom becomes more readily available to everyone.

By this point in the book, it should be increasingly obvious that every aspect of physical existence comprises of energy ... from the energy of thought, to the energy of matter, and of course the first physical energy ... *light* ... from which all other physical energy is derived except the first thought ... *let there be light!* Serenity is a composure of energy ... a quieting of the whirling planets which revolve around you, the central sun of your universe.

The exercise with which we will conclude this guide on happiness, will focus you on power, then serenity.

𝄞

Playing forceful classical music such as Beethoven's Fifth, at an enjoyable volume ...

Empty your head using TTM, and get the feeling of you being the centre of your universe. That is, *you* the being and not the false you of your mind. Sense the whirling surrounds of energy which exist around your viewpoint, and become sensitive to the etheric body which surrounds your physical body. You are the sun at the centre of your solar system and it is you who brings conscious life to all that is within your universe, as the solar sun does for our mutual physical universe. Feel that energy and acknowledge your power. Enjoy it and accept it. As you do this, begin the calming process which will lead you to a form of serenity. Calm. Calm. Calm the whirling planets and comfort the revolving dependencies. Calm them all and begin to enter into your inner world of serenity. Everything is calm and all is good. Once you have arrived, stay until you are confident of being able to find this place at any time, and under any circumstances. This is your inner world of mind, connected to the universal mind, and you have just contributed serenity into a place which needs it. Be still and KNOW.

... and so to a subject I call *the karma of empowerment and achievement* ...

the karma of empowerment and achievment

Guide Six
the karma of empowerment and achievement

Karma is the unerring law which adjusts effect to cause, on the physical, mental and spiritual planes of being ... H P Blavatsky

Diet

It is a well known fact amongst students of the Path, that spiritual progress beyond a certain point, will not tolerate the consumption of meat, alcohol or nicotine; in fact any drug or intoxicant is detrimental to truly achieved enlightenment. Note my words ... *beyond a certain point,* but I do not correlate such abstention with the *instigation of* spiritual progress, although it may well be the case for some.

To meat or not to meat, that is the question ... whether it be nobler to abstain, or irrelevant for the purposes of this work? Well, it is relevant, and to assess just how important the topic is, we need to study the *five kingdoms of life,* their relationship with each other, and the responsibilities each must accept for the other.

Each kingdom is evolving, and the dependents of today are the gods of tomorrow! *How* you imagine, that from an atom of dust, a consciousness will evolve, is for your imagination to tackle. For me, it is the only answer offered to me that has shone inner light on a difficult topic.

The mineral kingdom is down at the bottom right now, yet when it is composed into the form of an aircraft, it flirts with the Angels. The plant kingdom seems similarly unevolved, yet we eat from it and it is pleased to serve us by recomposing itself into our human bodies, thus serving the gods that are us. The animal kingdom gives us many companions, some of which are aware of the lower sub planes of the astral world, which is a place that may be utilised by highly evolved beings, who, because of their spiritual

163

progress are unable to manifest on earth; this sharing of space is a privilege.

The human kingdom is absolutely unique, in that it is the only known composite of individual spirit and single physical body. The human being, composed of spiritual, mental and physical elements, and capable of life on each of the corresponding planes, is capable of evolving during incarnation, to a state whereby it is able to know the mysteries of the universe, judge them, and choose to acknowledge or deny them.

The kingdom of God is within each and everyone of us. It is that divine spark which cannot ever be extinguished. We are sparks from a body of fire which released us, yet remained integral. This kingdom is available to the Being whilst incarnate, whose aspiration to live wholly within the fifth kingdom is alive.

Can you imagine someone further evolved along the evolutionary line to us humans, slitting your throat and eating you? What about killing by proxy and sending the heavenly butcher down to see you off? What would you think when overhearing a conversation at the ethereally anthropomorphic dinner table which sounded something like this ... *I like a nice piece of American's liver ... mmm the parson's nose ... that Korean meat tastes nicer when they terrify it before death ... drain the blood from those Israelis first ... stick the apple in that English girl's mouth ... boil him alive like he did the lobster ... baste her with butter made from the milk of her own breasts ... let me carve!*

Overboard? I don't think so!

We have now reached a stage in our process where the eating of meat and fish, or indeed eggs containing unborn life, is utterly contemptuous. It is such a gross form of underdevelopment, that it needs to be addressed and challenged as an overt folly of the

Aquarian Age. I see human carnivores in a similar light to that in which they see cannibals.

The logical nature of my discussion is simple and leads totally towards veganism; the eating of food which has caused neither pain nor death to the provider. Nuts are available, fruit is a gift, and most plants can be eaten. I know of some people however, who believe that we should not eat root vegetables such as parsnip and carrot, as the harvesting of them is painful to Mother Earth, much as it is to you when a hair is plucked from your head. *Whoaaa!!!* ... I hear you think; you have read this far without thinking me mentally deficient, so bear with me. Well, my role is to present alternatives and conclude workable methods for our trek along the success highway ... this is one such alternative that we are perhaps not ready to embrace?

To return practically and subjectively to the topic of diet, my Family and I are vegetarians, if we have to be pigeon holed, and have a pragmatic regimen not always to our liking, especially when dining out, but nevertheless workable. There is no end to the argument of pain and suffering caused in the survival methods of our race ... *is it fair to force grow a lettuce out of season in a glass house? ... is it right that tomatoes should be picked before fully grown?* Well, no, I think, or suppose, well, maybe, or not?? Yes, this is the type of mental dilemma which can be instigated when contemplating the issue. It lasts throughout spiritual progress ... unless you stop it!

You should get yourself into a situation where there is no attention on diet. Work your regimen so that you do not become it ... *she's a vegetarian ... he's a vegan ... we're all vegetarians, except we eat a bit of chicken now and then* ... are all examples of *self-compartmentalisation*. Is that all you are? No! Eating is merely a means of surviving, and never is nor ever shall be you. Dietary Karma is relevant in that the causing of pain and suffering as a cause emanation from you, will have to return and have its effect upon you. Ponder this concept into your life and enjoy any changes that may be stimulated into being.

SK

> May I inject an observation from a long forgotten philosopher ... this universe operates on the basic principle that life must ingest life to survive. Something must die for something else to live. This produces the universal game of eat or be eaten, and the impossibility of living without sinning or wronging, against other creatures of God. Therefore we are all sinners and need forgiveness, if we take other life for our own benefit. This associates with our table blessings, and savages who give thanks to the group spirit for the sacrifice of the animal s life to maintain their own. Whether this is *relevant,* as you say quite often Phil, is up to the individual reader.
>
> *... end of note*

I repeat that we are human, and have only, relatively recently, evolved to a stage whereby we have transcended the need to prey upon those weaker than ourselves. We must understand that it is silly to become bigoted and narrow; occasionally we will cause unnecessary harm to other forms of existence during our living process ... without becoming fixated, you may remedy such imbalance during the regular discourse of your life, without drawing undue attention to each and every deviation. Indeed, it is felt that if you honestly examine the events of a day at the end of it, and adjust any shortcomings displayed by yourself, repairing any damage and making relevant amends, this will allow your *between lives* experience to be far more blissful than may otherwise be the case.

As the hyena *eats* a meal, it constantly scans surroundings to ensure it does not *become* a meal. We are not comfortable with such insecurity and I advise you to address the issue of diet with this in mind. As progress is made along the Path, natural

166

adjustments will find their way into your regular patterns of existence; some you will be conscious of and others you will not.

Moving onwards, I ask you to contemplate the priority on your list of dietary requirements, and suggest that you consider oxygen. It is the element which will kill you more quickly through its absence, than anything else will in its presence. Exercise to oxygenate all those tiny capillaries waiting patiently at the end of each toe for this life giving gas. Avoid toxic situations which are poisonous because of their very lack of this vital element. Breathe fresh air and ensure your surroundings are forever healthful of this elemental ally.

Eat live food ... not alive food!

Consume fresh vegetables that have avoided our compulsion to process away their goodness in a factory. Avoid tins, frozen comestibles and indeed any other form of preserved food whenever possible. There is no real need for it, and it is only your habits and laziness which will prevent you from instigating progress into this aspect of your existence.

There is an ancient magic formula which is no longer sorcery to our advanced viewpoints. If you can maintain any new behaviour pattern for the full duration of a moon cycle, then it will inculcate its way into your tendencies of its own accord. This process is similar to etching on glass; the pattern is inlaid on to the subconscious, *which is ruled by the moon,* and becomes part of you. This etching is even stronger if the desired new behaviour pattern is begun at the time of the new moon, because it is believed that any efforts started at that time will be completed or assured of success, by the full moon of that cycle. Sounds like an old wives tale but it works. Living on earth means that you have a strong cyclical relationship with moon periods, which last approximately twenty nine and a half days. Try this old trick and see if it works for you.

Alcohol uses oxygen and vitamins in its role as an intoxicant, which would otherwise be available for your bodies natural healing capabilities. Drugs can instill a temporary awareness in an individual, of possibilities and vistas not hitherto contemplated. Drug experiences are all but useless in any quest for spiritual gain and must be discarded to the rubbish heap. They keep you in an *effect state,* rather than the *cause state* which this book recommends to you. Each new plateau of awareness available, can only be achieved permanently through will, determination, service to others and clean living. I need not embrace the subject of nicotine and smoking here ... some people I know still indulge; a healer friend of mine in Australia, actually started smoking when she began her healing career. She is not to be mentored on this subject however, and would be the first to agree with me. You must ever bear in mind that you have a responsibility not to kill your body just as you have in the preservation of other life.

You the divine flame will live forever, but it is the positive and mental aspects of life on earth that allow you physical consciousness. For this we need bodies, and your responsibility is with yours, as well as others. Smoking kills! If that is what you stand for then do it if you must. That is a beauty of our type of existence ... you are forever your own judge and jury. You decide if you are guilty, but take an oath against your own divinity before you conclude the trial.

Whatever you do within the sphere of dietary improvement, ensure that you adopt my rule of *gradual graduation* towards any change. You will notice a resultant and gradual self-access available, to your reservoir of energy, in direct proportion to your adoption of healthful habits. Even if you do not wish to instigate immediate change, then it is as well you know about possibilities, which, at an appropriate time in your living process, will manifest in consciousness giving you further opportunity to embrace their possibilities.

There is an excellent and thought provoking book called *The Secret Life of Your Cells,* which describes in dubious scientific detail, the awareness existing in each and every cell of your body. It shows that cells taken from a body, react even when removed and transported great distances, to any threatening behaviour exhibited towards the main body of cells they have left behind.

This group awareness is related to collective utilisation of matter. The matter we use for the composition of bodies, belongs to a group reservoir ... *ashes to ashes, dust to dust* ... just as the matter we use for thought belongs to the mind stuff reservoir, much the same as the vital spark which is you, is part of a spiritual reservoir which is *not separate* from all the other divine sparks given off by the main body of light.

When you cease utilising a thought, the substance returns to the reservoir. We are all using the same materials and it is obvious that if desired, we can be conscious to a greater or lesser extent, of other uses of the same stuff. This is background data to another far sighted theory which states that plants are demonstrably conscious, in that they will react to threats. It is well known that some Nazis practiced black magic, and just as a Silent Knight flows love and forgiveness, they would train their minds by flowing hatred to a flower, and they graduated from that process when they could make the flower wilt through thought power.

If this consciousness exists, which I naturally believe to be the case, then it is wise also to treat plants with respect. The book that I have mentioned suggests that a plant possesses a natural tranquiliser which it administers to itself when threatened ... if you are about to kill it for the purpose of food, then give it warning, and it will render itself unconscious thus avoiding pain, and be very pleased to be utilised by the human god in this way.

Please do not mistakenly judge all consciousness subjectively by your own level of achievement. The gradient scale is active here as it is everywhere. The consciousness of a plant, which is the manifestation of a group spirit controlling many such actualities, would be akin to a dreamless sleep in a human. Pain and pleasure within such organisms must be judged with this in mind, but not as an exoneration for ill treatment. The karma of diet must be embraced realistically ... it is impossible to humanly exist without creating negative karma, as our friend a Silent Knight mentioned earlier ... do not use this fact as an excuse; rather, cherish it as a stimulus for improvement

Denials, Affirmations, Referrals, Mantrams and Inculcations

There is no doubt about the fact that you can improve your life by the power of positive suggestion. Much as a life can be ruined by stray thoughts of shortcomings, and third party insistence that you are a certain ineffectual way, it can also be turned around to your advantage utilising the same mechanisms which are being used against most people for detrimental ends.

The rule of the universe relevant to this section of writing, is a powerful phrase which I have understood in many different formations, but none so effectual as can be found in the *blue books* written by Alice Bailey. **Energy Follows Thought,** is how the Tibetan Djwhal Khul eloquently portrays the concept in these books, and if you practice, you will discover such words to be helpful, pragmatic and true. Likewise, if you do not practice, then the power of the mind will become almost similar to the fictitious robot of the future, which has no further need for its master, and demonstrates this independence by working against the survival of them both through ignorance.

A thought *is* form.

Most of us are only able to create relatively weak thought forms, which soon dissipate as their source of creation turns attention towards something else. Quite often however, if there is little opposition to a weak thought form, then it will physically manifest, and its creator will wondrously announce magic! Weak thought forms are also *additive*. That is, many weak but similar thought forms from many different minds over the entire planet, attract each other, thus becoming a tremendous source of power, either good or bad. This is exactly why there is so much of the negative thought power in existence, often exacerbated by the news profession, who have made up a law of their own which states ... *if it bleeds, it leads*. This outlook does not help the cause of planetary harmony, and it is partly the reason why a Silent Knight pleads to the world ... *whoever you are, wherever you are, think of the words LOVE and FORGIVENESS, every time you find yourself with some idle time to do so.*

The sheer weight of uncontrolled and selfish thought that exists on the astral plane, usually ensures deviation or destruction of weak thought form however, and this fact alone often works to the benefit of their creators ... if the thoughts of most were to come true, then God alone knows what would be the fate of parents, children, friends, colleagues, bosses, animals and even selves!

I feel like death ... I am so ugly ... my backside is huge ... I am so stupid ... nothing ever goes right for me ... everyone works against me ... can you imagine if those sentiments were allowed to manifest in their pristine flavours, immediately. Even the faintest thought about anything has power however, and we must agree on that fact if you are to obtain maximum benefits from this work. Many of these weaker forms manifest in the inner world of mind belonging to their creator, and it is there that they fester and develop power through the repetitive procedure of constant reflection. People think themselves into a certain mould, and usually do not know that they are doing it.

You idiot ... you are so slow ... you look ill ... you are your own

171

worst enemy ... you won't get on with that attitude ... she gives me a pain in the .... are all examples of what another thinks about someone, who may well take each suggestion on board and be that way for a variety of reasons. These second person suggestions, as I call them, are often powerful in direct proportion to the significance which the utterer has within the life of the recipient.

Your inner world of mind is a control mechanism of unthinkable power, yet it can be brought down by simple and insipid suggestion, rendered totally ineffectual as the inherent tool of good fortune which it most definitely is, and can even become a friendly enemy of the worst order. It is sometimes likened to a parasite which inadvertently kills its host, and in so doing renders death inevitable for itself as its source of food decays.

Any practical guide to personal success must disseminate mind power as the major contributor towards full achievement of goals and happiness. I heartily recommend you to begun a fuller study of mind power after reading this book a couple of times. Your inspiration may come from a regimented teaching or a more mystical and poetic source. Always remember that your goal is senior to any emotional response you may exhibit towards the teachings.

✎

For poetic inspiration I recommend James Allen's little book, *As a Man Thinketh*. Although written in the late nineteenth century, it is widely available in many forms from miniature, to full size hardback. The stapled edition is the least expensive, and there is even an edition which has been rewritten in an affirmation style. I recommend the original however! If you enjoy exercises then a course in *Raja Yoga* will help, in either book form, or as lessons in a classroom. Personalities have nothing to do with benefits, and I recommend you avoid anything popularly built around the fame of an individual. Ageless wisdom has no price, and it is only the practicalities of modern day living which force money to be exchanged, often in the form of registration fees, or voluntary contributions towards expenses.

In this book we are going to illustrate ways and means by which you can change your life through changing your mind. Without studying the innermost workings, I suggest you begin control with *Denials*.

⋏

Pick a thought that has been recurring in your mind, and decide to control it. Then, much as you may twist and scrunch up a newspaper when it no longer serves any useful purpose for you, do the same with this thought. Thank it for its service, and suggest it finds its way back to the central reservoir of thought stuff. Now, once you begin playing with this thought matter, you will discover methods that most suit you for such control. I deny power to anything in my inner world, except under my authority, before proceeding to the more positive stages of affirmation.

You are an outpost of consciousness, serving perceptions of the greater whole. There are no restraints whatsoever, placed upon your behaviour, and this is all part of the gathering of information for the body from which we were breathed, sometimes called *The All*. Such description of initial conception, which I have just made, are for the purpose of divine stimulation within you. A concept will gradually manifest into your awareness over the years, which will allow ever greater glimpses of divinity. The more progress you make in every day life, the quicker such glimpses may come into being.

Positive *Affirmations* offer a quick and simple process by which

173

you will be able to force feed your life with change. I have already suggested one earlier in this book ... *I am Happy!* I always recommend the customisation of affirmations, just as I also understand that few of us make the effort. PAC People use affirmations ... PAC Practitioners write their own ... and Advanced PAC Practitioners enjoy the benefits of previously affirmed sentiments whilst honing the finer edges of nuance within each. I offer you the following suggestions, and hope you progress quickly on towards writing your own. Remember to affirm in the present tense, as if what you want to have happen already has! What you affirm is immediately manifested in your *thought* world ... its physical counterpart can be thought of similarly to something you have *bought* by mail order ... you know that it will be received eventually. Say them out aloud then think them, alternately. Repetition is the key to success in this department. Concentration focuses more attention units onto what you desire, and gives more life to the thought form. Some affirmations are in the first, and others in the second person, as if you are being told by others that you are a certain way. My second book *Before the Beginning is a Thought,* contains detachable cards which can help in your affirmation of the positive.

♪

Play your favourite inspirational classical music in the background.

↑

I am a winner ... I have lots of money ... I know what I want ... you always get things done ... I love my Family ... you are clever ... I am serendipity ... you turn bad into good ... I am successful ... you are happy ... you are a good friend ... I see a bright future ... you know what you want ... I am loving ...

Play around with these affirmations and get them to work for you. *Change the I's into You's and the You's into I's ... the My's into Your's and the Your's into My's.* I am sure you get the idea. As you begin working with mental matter, you will discover that all is not necessarily well defined in terms of wants and not wants, likes and dislikes, directions and aspirations. *Referrals* are self explanatory and work in a similar fashion to a pending tray in an office. You may need more information from either your inner source, or an external origin of data, before you decide on a course of mental action. By all means refer, but not as an excuse for indecision.

I differentiate qualities of mental work by utilising varying nomenclature. When I cease asking for material possessions in my life and aspire towards certain human merits I utilise *Mantrams.* It is the same technique which I have already described, but you will notice that the sentiment is far from similar. Mantrams, like mantra as a word, is derived from the Sanskrit *man,* which means *to think.* It is mainly used by Hindus as an inward chant during meditation, and is further proof of the valid link between the ageless wisdom and modern day personal development. A mantram is simply a word or phrase that when repeated, influences the human mind. A well known mantram would be *Aum mani padme hum,* where you would blend the end into the beginning of the repeat. I use understandable English words for our purposes, although it is possible to achieve a change of state by pure repetition of an otherwise incomprehensible phrase. You may like background music or not, depending on your disposition. It is optional; as you repeat my examples which follow soon, get acquainted with the concept, and then compose your own mantrams.

It is said that words have spiritual and material components. The spiritual parts are the vowels, and the material parts are the consonants. *All intelligible words ... sounds uttered and symbols written ...* when thought, voiced or inscribed, produce thought

175

forms with which we are familiar. The thought form, however, is not a *word* in the ether, but a very recognizable *representation of the word,* regardless of the language used. A simple example would be the words boy in English, *chico* in Spanish and *puer* in Latin ... all would collect or connect together on the thought form represented by the concept we know as *boy.* They would *vibrate and resonate* the same way in the Ether Waves. This can explain why language is no barrier in telepathy and most healing. Notice I said *intelligible words.* There are also unintelligible *sounds and symbols* which have their corresponding thought forms, and notice that the mantrams are predominantly made up of vowel sounds. *AUM* is entirely vowel in sound, if we allow M s and N s as not *pure* consonants. The thought forms represented by such chanting of *vowels* we may never fathom, but we can at least now see that they *are* spiritual, and have them make a bit more sense to our questioning minds.

I will also mention that *rhythm* in music is material and melody is spiritual. Why? The explanation is connected to heartbeat, which is a sign of material *life.* Speed of rhythm indicates the level of the active life at a particular time. This explains the effectiveness of using rhythm-*less* music in meditation recordings.

These mechanical explanations for abstractions are often very effective with many people, and are frequently precursors to *real* acceptance and understanding of some of this *higher plane* stuff.

§K

I visited a Borderland Researcher called Peter Lindemann. I was asking about a machine called the *Pulsed Scalar Resonator* that he was building. He said it affected the etheric body by producing beneficial vibrations for it. There was much more to his explanation, but irrelevant for our purpose here. I questioned him as to how he knew which vibrations were beneficial. He replied that he used the words vibration, frequency or wave length, because our language does not have a word or words to describe the differences in *thought forms* ... as we do in radio waves! I pursued further explanation by telling him that I still did not fully understand. He continued ... *thought forms are fourth dimensional and are kind of like three dimensional shapes. The numbers of different shapes are infinite. How does one sort them into high and low on a numerical scale? To our minds it is an impossible task ... perhaps someday a computer will do it for us ... the only thing we can state that makes sense is to say that **like thought forms vibrate on the same wave length or frequency,** and accept the fact that we really are using misnomers* ... Can you see how new this is, and the huge area for expanding our understanding which is opening up in this field?

... *end of note.*

... as promised, the mantrams ...

↑

I am filled with love ... I am conscious of my intrinsic spirituality ... I feel my relationship to the planet ... my mind is in tune with Divine Purpose ... I acknowledge the great reservoirs of matter, mind substance and spirit ... I am master of my own mind ... I am at a level of cause over my inner and outer worlds ... I am a centre of divine consciousness ... I am ... I am ... I am ...

There are quite a number of I AM groups in existence; they are separate for the same reasons we have Baptists, Methodists and Calvinists. Their practical philosophy is usually based around the thrice repeated end sentiment I have just used, *I am.* They are simple and powerful words which emphasise the self as *I,* and reality as *am.* These words alone can help steer a course towards at-one-ness. The alignment of the spiritual, mental and physical vehicles is uppermost in the teachings of most great world religions, and any efforts which you make of your own accord, should be profitable in terms of spiritual progress.

It is *not* wise, to contemplate in any depth, the fact that your spiritual progress will inevitably lead you into a denial of the need, for the very possessional aspirations which introduced you to the world of personal development in the first place The paradox reigns supreme for much of the divine voyage. At this moment of your journey, it may deter you from continuing, yet there comes a milestone on the Path, where attachment to the material world becomes less significant.

I have always denied the need for spiritual progress to be shown in terms of poverty, material restriction, no physical ambition, no car, no house, no business, no job, no prospects, no fun, no money ... in fact I call such exhibition *the big no!* Perhaps there was a time when this attitude was relevant, but not any longer.

Balance is the goal whilst incarnate! *Yang Yin,* in Tao, means being on the little bridge which spans the two dots, or seeds, in the two interlocking commas of this Chinese symbol. Also the *caduceus symbol* in medicine, with the wings at the top and the two serpents *Ida* and *Pengali* intertwining at the seven chakra points is also perhaps indicative of balance. The little circle at the top and the wings symbolise the freed soul. I wonder how many doctors know this?

Divine and prosper, I exhort!

Avoid the temptation to state an attachment of your particular goals to celestial command, as they did in the days of the Crusades. If you are level headed, and understand that you should not profit through the ageless wisdom *at someone elses expense,* then, as I once heard Cliff Richard sing ... *why should the devil have all the good music?*

This time of incarnation is to be enjoyed and not endured! The body is a temple for you to live in. The planet is where you can care for the lesser kingdoms. The astral world is where yourself and others may control wayward desire. The mental world is *the developing world,* where others are waiting to help you. The spirit world is home.

SK

> A clear delineation should be made here between *spirit world* and *the world of spirits* for those who are new to this information. There is a *world* of difference! Pun intended!
> ... end of note.

I believe that we have reached a time period where increasing numbers of incarnate souls understand that balance is the order of this new age that is upon us. A friend of mine drew a cross for me ... at the top he wrote *spirit,* at the bottom he wrote *matter,* to the left he wrote *negative* and to the right he wrote *positive.* That central point where these four manifestations meet, is the ideal point for a human being to dwell, he suggested. Think of this balanced cross and see if it inspires a pleasing thought. With such balance in mind, as in my previous book, *Before the Beginning is a Thought,* I prescribe *Inculcations.*

Affirmative Inculcations

I specially searched for a suitable word to describe the pleasing indoctrination of a beneficial nature ... I knew it had to have ancient tones and a poetic etymology ... in Latin, *inculcatus* is the past participle of *inculcare;* they are both derived from *calcare,* which means *to tread,* and this word in turn comes from *calx* which means *heel.* I immediately had visions of the old Romans treading grapes with their feet whilst chanting beneficial slogans. I define inculcation as meaning, *to trample into the mind by way of repetition.*

Inculcations must be balanced ... Affirmations are just for you the human being ... Mantrams are with you, the Divine Being, in mind ... and Affirmative Inculcations are available to serve you, the

Being here on earth, as a workable formula with which you may impress upon your mind whatever you wish to become, have, hear, see, do, go and give. The power is in the balance! Nature abhors a vacuum, and a natural outflow always precedes an otherwise spontaneous inflow. If you know this to be true, then I urge you to begin this balancing act with outflow. The Affirmative Inculcation is very much a tool of the Advanced PAC Practitioner, who always benefits by knowledge of natural law.

⁂

> Service to others is always important ... smiling at friends is a gift from the heart ... my thoughts are effective, I control them wisely ... developing skills is a goal which I cherish ... I am a channel for light ... I am a channel for love ... I am a channel for power ... I am wealthy ... all that is mine belongs to others also ... my good health shines onto my friends ... I attract purity as a good fortune magnet ... I discard worn out habits and introduce more kindness ... I understand the great reservoirs theory ... I use all the matters and return them with knowingness ... I meet all my needs with high spirits and thoughtfulness ... I am at one with the greater whole ... I support all that is good ... my Family and I prosper, every day in every way ... I am master of my own destiny ... I create good fortune ... I mould a great future ... I visualise peace on earth ... I am a loving pink flow of energy ... my gifts are abundant and natural ... I am a deep blue flow of knowledge ... I learn ... I am ... I am ... I am!

As you can gather from the flavour of Affirmative Inculcations, they cover a wide variety of sentiments, yet the balance between giving and receiving always remains. The whole of creation as we understand it, is based around cyclical routines of inflow and outflow ... egress and ingress ... stopping and starting with change in between. This complete book is based on personal success being a microcosm of the greater cosmic example which is seen to work!

If you are to prosper from this knowledge, which I urge you to so do, then you must continue your studies of *The Divine Cosmic Plan* in any way that is real to you.

I learn something new each day, as I focus on the grand scheme of things. Every piece of data is not always immediately relevant to the particular process I am existing with at that moment, yet as long as my source material is honourable, each particle of data usually finds its place in my life at some point in time. Affirmative Inculcations are a tool which now allows you to precisely manipulate your existence into the super league. Use each new theme for a moon cycle at the very least, and watch the sentiment become you. I must now inculcate the lesson of ...

Catalytic Comprehension!

Faith uses attention units to hold onto certain thought forms which you may or may not have control over, and is the single most evident common denominator which can be sampled as tangible in every success story which we are allowed to examine. Determination is a close relative, and together, they form the mental equivalent of a physical TNT explosion. These two qualities are long known and understood in the world of personal development, yet they still find their way into this book which is a modern blend of ageless wisdom into modern day life. Why? Because faith and determination were two early parts of the esoteric formulae which were released for general exoteric consumption. If they had been abused to the detriment of the planet, then other more powerful ingredients would *not* have followed quite so quickly, although *all* will have to be revealed eventually.

Do not misunderstand me by thinking that I preach success as being unobtainable without these occult revelations. It is ... for the few that inadvertently stumble onto it, or those who follow the rules unknowingly. Revelation merely makes something which is already in existence, known. Buddha did not invent exteriorisation, he discovered the possibility. Christ did not create life after death, he exposed it to be so through a demonstration of phenomena.

Catalytic comprehension is an understanding of the physical and spiritual elements, which the modern alchemist utilises to blend with goals and aspirations, thus creating PAC Magic. Faith is an abstract idea of commitment. You can manifest faith in your mental universe and it will be physically visible to you as a concept. A whirling of energy, a moulding of the fine mental ether, a mental commitment to the success of any given venture. Faith is of paramount importance ... it can heal ... it can kill ... it will force ... it is fire ... it is knowing!

Faith has many guises, which can be illustrated by a story, of the man whose house was flooded when the banks of a nearby river collapsed. He was firstly warned to evacuate his dwelling by the local policeman; as the waters rose, a fireman called to ask if he needed help; the water level forced him upstairs at which point a representative of the Navy arrived by boat and pleaded with him to leave the house; an Army officer called him by loud hailer asking if all was well; the last dry place available to him was the chimney pot, and on this he sat as an Air Force helicopter hovered overhead begging him to grab the rope and evacuate a house which was sure to be engulfed within seconds. To each of his potential rescuers, he had replied to their offers of help that *God would save him!*

He drowned, and after a short while in Heaven he saw God. He summoned up enough courage for a confrontation and asked, *tell me God, I had faith in you, why did you not come and save me?"*

"Faith? Save you? I sent the Police, Fire Brigade, Army, Navy and even an Air Force helicopter to save you and you took no notice!" was God's reply.

Faith is the first element which must be utilised in this science of catalytic comprehension. It must be kept apart from any ideas which you are currently contemplating, until you are certain you want them manifested in the physical universe.

Picture the goal on a crucible; see faith in a pipette ...

They are both quite ineffectual. Pour the contents of the pipette into the crucible, and a phantom manifests ... it is an ether of energy with a will of its own, alive in a world of fine substance which becomes denser with each thought of the blend. Can you be responsible for this spectre? If you cannot, then do not! I write factually and not poetically. This is an accurate description of creation, which I have purposely left until this late part of the book.

Picture the goal on a crucible; see faith in a pipette; then channel determination to the crucible as you blend faith with the goal!

As with everything, determination has its origin in your inner mental realms. Once created in the fine ethers of mind stuff *continuously,* then can you physically determine whatever outcome you wish. The dangers inherent in this knowledge are not always apparent to the naive apprentice magician ... Advanced PAC Practitioners are not ever naive in their transcendence from PAC culture into the realms of apprentice magicianhood. White magic is ever the end for PAC Transcendees and all those possessing honourable aim; it is impossible in all but the fewest cases to achieve Advanced PAC Practitioner status without your goals being shiny white. Ignorance is inexcusable to the white aspirant who wanders onto the paths less well lit. Understand this, and note the little space taken up by the formulae in this book, compared to the pages devoted to warnings. If you ever use this knowledge for the destruction of another, the karmic wheel will turn on you with a blast equivalent to that which you utilised to create in evil.

I have introduced you to the centre of creation, and now I will turn your attention to the more physical aspects of staying on course. A positive mental attitude is a prerequisite for all achievement, and if you are prepared to *always give over and above* what is expected from you, then that quality will contribute a good and beneficial flow from others, in your direction. You must be willing to discipline yourself; all the time this alchemical creation we earlier described, is being held in thought within your mental universe, you will be unable to follow any previously unconnected courses of action in both business and leisure activities. This will cause an imbalance in your life which is to be avoided. Periodically, you must address this possibility, and, whilst still holding your goal firmly in place within your inner worlds, you must release yourself from physical bondage to it, and relax into an unrelated pastime.

Other people are often the only visible division between the two radical shades of magic. Black magic is for selfish gain at the expense of others, and white magic is performed for the benefit of all. PAC Magic allows personal gain in the service of others. The ability to work with others is a mark of the right way of thinking, although this fact should not be used to forge false relationships. The equation which I calculated in *You Can Always Get What You Want* was $1 + 1 = 3$. This still holds true as do all natural phenomena, and refers to the fact that when one mind joins together with another in mutually beneficial aim, a third force is created, the qualities of which will not be found totally in either instigator. This is a principle known as *Gestalt,* and is also the esoteric meaning of the Holy Trinity, which still baffles many priests and other religious leaders. This third gestalt force is a sum which cannot be reduced to its constituent parts. In order to create such beneficial gestalts, it is necessary to contemplate the inclusion of others within both your plans and modus operandi. This involvement will propel you towards the enjoyment of mutual and beneficial PAC Magic, as you transcend your sphere of operation

184

into the realms of PAC Alchemy.

Attention is a catalyser of magnificent proportions, and a cultivation of concentration will bring with it far reaching benefits. Concentrated attention acts as a magnifying glass does with the sun's rays. Attention units are *life-givers* to your thoughts. If solar energy is channelled through a glass, it will heat the area it is focussed upon to the point of fire. This is the same as concentrated attention of thought ... if you channel it ... stunning force is created.

A good memory is helpful in any quest for success, and the information necessary for this faculty is gained most expediently through attention. It will be found that even in the most senile of our elderly citizens, memory will usually be recallable to the degree that attention was concentrated at the time of exposure to the facts waiting to be recalled. Thus, memories are available from long ago when attention was concentrated, yet senility prevents such people from recalling what they had for breakfast. If your memory is not good however, do not worry about it, as this worry could be as damaging to your health as a good memory would be to your achievement possibilities!

⅄

Concentrate your attention onto the tip of a ball point pen for thirty seconds. Increase the time span on this exercise daily, by further increments of thirty seconds. Cease the routine when you can concentrate in this manner for one hour, without intrusive thoughts of any description. If this exercise is not appealing to you, or you find it too difficult, remember the *gradual graduation* rule ... it may take some readers a lifetime or more to achieve such concentration for an hour! The positive aspect of any concentration inabilities you may discover lurking within, is the fact that you now know *how to,* and *when* is only a matter of time!

185

Your ability to creatively visualise the finished outcome of personal activities, will have obvious bearing on the accuracy of achievement. Creative visualisation is a much misunderstood activity in this day and age where it is endemic for almost everyone to aspire towards a career in the arts or media. Let me tell you that it is possible to be an absolute failure in the creative arts aspect of human existence, yet be an *enfant terrible* in the inner world of mind, where creative visualisation occurs. I have illuminated the way, and it is through TTM that the inner room for creative visualisation will be discovered.

Mental matter is a flimsy substance which can change form at an alarming pace. To that degree it is quite unlike physical matter. In your inner world of mind it is thought concentration which keeps an object in manifestation; in the outer world it is gravity and objectivity.

Picture a house ... mock it up within five seconds to your own design, then explode it into fragments as the sixth second strikes. Obviously, do not try to do that in the physical universe quickly, or at all, as it cannot be done. Ponder the significance of this comparison, and illuminate the concepts of creative visualisation and thought concentration.

It is a symptom of spiritual development to be penniless. This is an outdated fancy, and as I have already mentioned, the ascetics of yesterday are the high flying business executives of today. Work on budgets for every aspect of your life and live according to the writings of Charles Dickens, who equated in one of his books, outgoings exceeding income with misery, and income exceeding outgoings with happiness.

Mistakes are an important part of your future, but this should in

186

no way encourage you to make them. Rather, such negative feedback should help you utilise the experience already gained from those moments of bitter disappointment which have happened to us all. I remember a story of the executive who offered his resignation after making *a million pound mistake*. The chairman refused to accept it stating that he had just made *a million pound investment* in the executive's training! This is a good and positive allegorical example for dealing with such accidents. It is also an excellent illustration of the *half full - half empty* aspects of positive and negative attitudes.

The employment of music as an aid to assimilation of material, is widely used now that the theories of left and right brain distinctions have been successfully disseminated. In the eighteenth century, Johann Sebastian Bach discovered at the instigation of the Russian Count Kayserling, that after composing a *bright, interesting, but calm,* piece of music which was subsequently played by a harpsichord player called Johann Goldberg, that the Count's insomnia was cured. This is what the Count wanted from that exercise, but research continued in the early 1970s by the Bulgarian scientist Dr Georgi Lozanov, proved that such music could instill a variety of desirable states within the human being. Some theories postulate that it is the rhythm which is beneficial, and others believe in the music itself. Whatever the belief, enjoyable music played at sixty beats per minute is relaxing and most definitely assists in the mental absorption of anything, including sleep. Baroque music of this nature by Bach, Vivaldi, Telemann, Corelli and Handel, is suitable for the purpose of study, creative visualisation, affirmative inculcations and *sheer enjoyment* ... let us not forget this latter purpose for music!

Autogenic Training is a form of creative visualisation, and was seen to be particularly effective in the areas of self confidence and sports. The idea of competitive sport is becoming less and less appealing, as the enjoyment of events by participants recedes into the distant background. Why do we continue to call it sport when pleasure has taken a back seat and the winning team is nearly always the one who has the highest paid manager and players? It is nevertheless of importance to note scientific influence of any description within our lives, and it is a fact that baroque music increased the efficiency of autogenic training. I mention this as scientific evidence of that which I recommend. I am sure you have also seen reports in connection with the psyching up of an athlete's skill, by mentally visualising the desired performance many times, and always with positive results ... *sinking the long putt* ... *hitting the basket* ... *ace-serving in tennis* ... *scoring the goal in soccer.*

𝄞

Music lifts the spirits ... the dawn of all known creation was begun by the utterance of a musical note ... *the note sounded forth!* Please keep to the forefront of your thoughts, the fact that it exists to be enjoyed. With this in mind, it can also be utilised as I have described. I suggest you find a baroque piece at around sixty beats per minute, which is to your liking, and then play it to accompany the following exercise. It is not mere coincidence that this beat is a nice, quiet, calming influence on most people, as it is the speed of heart beat for most of us when we are relaxed. Rhythm in music, as I have already mentioned, is psychologically identified with heart beat which equates with the majority, to *life.* No heart beat and absence of rhythm equals *death,* or at least a state of other worldness, and correlates to the sort of rhythm-*less,* flowing nature of most meditation music. I have mentioned this again because the field of music is full of occult connotations which our inner being recognises; as is *colour.* Both are fields in themselves to be pondered further by the individual.

Using the goal which you wrote down during the past life exercise contained in guide five ... in a pleasing room where you will not be disturbed for one hour ... picture that goal on a crucible, see faith in a pipette, then channel determination to the crucible as you blend faith with the goal! Mould the combinations in mental matter, before adding the whirling mists of faith and determination into the blend. Concentrate your attention onto this procedure and repeat the routine as you did the exercise with the ball point pen ... through *gradual graduation,* focus your concentrated attention for longer and longer, until you are able to keep your creation in mental matter alive at all times!

Ponder the process, and in so doing, check that your purpose has remained honourable.

Write down the benefits which will become apparent to others during the accomplishment of this goal. If you have wavered in your outlook on service, then re-instill the virtues of giving, and may this ever be to the forefront of your mind!

By now, if you have followed my instructions, and blended them with the most important of ingredients which can only be found inside of you ... the personal goal ... you should be feeling *a degree* of empowerment. You have knowledge of the intellect and heart and you are aware of the need to align heart centres with mind centres. You are cognisant of the human being as a microcosm of the macrocosm, and no doubt, you are grateful to the wise of old who have cherished and guarded these data throughout the most horrific of onslaughts, including the Spanish Inquisition and the downfall of Atlantis.

Some information under the category of ageless wisdom, was available in days of yore, and it merely ceased to be fashionable as great civilisations perished. When the Romans eventually left Britain, it was not until the nineteenth century that bathing once more became acceptable. The Romans had promoted cleanliness as a virtue, so *that* actuality was immediately thrown out with all the other instigations of the aggressors, rather than being cherished as the positive amongst the negative.

The Egyptians were aware of themselves as microcosms of the universe, and followed astrological guidelines in their behaviour. They acknowledged the consciousness within their own organs and understood that nothing knows how to do the job of *a liver,* better than *a liver,* and they attributed this fact to organic intelligence. This data along with many of their beliefs, almost died alongside the Egyptian Empire.

The Atlanteans possessed psychic powers of the lower animal nature, and during those times, angels still walked amongst men. Kings were often Divine Beings sent to guide evolution along its weary way. The magic available to this civilisation was abused in a darker and darker fashion, until eventually they were wiped out as a root race; but not before they had left many reminders of their race behind, including the Pyramids, the Easter Island Statues, Stonehenge and many other huge structures. You see the Atlanteans were the giants spoken of in the Bible, just as was the flood which virtually wiped them out. Sometimes twenty seven feet tall, the building of monolithic structures to them, was comparable to the erection of a new church by us now.

Still existing are remnant genes which occasionally throw up the odd seven or eight feet human being even now. It takes many thousands of years for all traces of any civilisation to disappear. If you care to study occult history, you will find much to interest you ... the breaching of the Straits of Gibraltar by the Atlantic Ocean resulted in the Mediterranean Sea. Some remains of that dry land are the mountain peaks now known as the Spanish Balearic Islands. That should spice up interest during your next vacation to Menorca.

Easter Island, which is actually near the west coast of South America, was the eastern most point of land on the great continent of Lemuria. Also known as Mu, it was another destroyed continent that pre-dated Atlantis. St Helena and Ascension Island are reminders to the west of the destruction of Atlantis. If you wish to know what the Lemurians and possibly the Atlanteans looked like, then a study of the already mentioned statues on Easter Island will show you.

In the main, planet earth is currently populated by products of the fifth root race, and from this race will emerge the fifth kingdom of nature, which is the spiritual kingdom of God, under the great esoteric law of correspondence. It is widely predicted that the seeds for the dawning of the sixth root race are to be found in the United States of America ... that great melting pot of cultures born of dissatisfaction on many other parts of the globe. There will be seven root races before this earthly existence will have outlasted its usefulness as experience.

We have been involving for around eighteen million years, and as we are just past the lower most point of involution, and now on the upturn of evolution, it is perhaps fair to postulate another eighteen million years before this current process will be behind us. I speak of this only as an effort to stimulate thought, and to propel you towards ever increasing amounts of future gratifying achievement. It is such background data that helps contemplation beyond the norm, and it is those of us engaged in such pastimes that are capable of dreaming the dreams which will create the Heaven of tomorrow.

Karma will be ever present as the law of cause and effect, and it may very well be that you are prevented from the achievement of your dreams in their purist form because of past misdemeanors. It is also pertinent to contemplate success as a combination of past good deeds alongside present skill and judgement. *The karma of empowerment and achievement cannot ever interfere with the outflow of goodness.* You may have to fight through many evil intentions that still exist within your inner and outer worlds to achieve this outflow; and persist you must. Do not judge yourself by one lifetime alone, as this is an unnecessary cruelty to inflict upon yourself. Likewise, bad karma cannot ever be utilised as an excuse for indolence, *amongst those with the knowledge!*

Go forward, with a feel from the past, an eye to the future and your mind in the now! Dream the dreams ... light the light ... be the fire ... touch the power ... think the thought ... climb the peak ... support the strong ... help the weak!

I invite you to flick the switch marked Empowerment. It is within us all and waits only for a touch of inner world thought to manifest all you ever dreamed of being ...

⇨

empowerment

When the soul sees itself as a Center surrounded by its circumference - when the Sun knows that it is a Sun, surrounded by its whirling planets - then is it ready for the Wisdom and Power of the Masters ... *Yogi Ramacharaka*

Enablement

Continuity of consciousness should be a short term goal for all of us engaged in the process of aspiration towards full human development. It is a high goal and a lofty ideal when first contemplated, yet the dawning of possibilities is often just a short step away. To begin with, the term consciousness is a little misleading, as we are all continuously conscious, and it is only a question of whether or not we retain the information perceived during *un*consciousness, that causes us to believe that a new state has been achieved or not.

The word *awareness* is perhaps more appropriate, yet even that term conjures visions of abilities, and perceptions of new vistas, not necessarily associated with the ability to consciously perceive twenty four hours per day. You have the option of nomenclature, but I will continue with the most widely understood *continuity of consciousness* phrase for our purposes.

If you are healthy, drug free and a partaker of pure foods, exercise and fresh air, it is a fair bet for an esoteric gambler that you sleep well; providing your conscience is reasonably clear. Of course sleep time is anything but restful for the service industries of human bodies; rather, it is a time for action and renewal whilst the will is free of corporeal qualification. If you choose to eat late, and find that your meal has not digested before sleep, then you will have wasted energy better utilised elsewhere, for the assimilation of nutrients ... an activity designed to be accomplished during waking hours!

We have discussed a variety of awareness states, and almost all of them must inevitably lead a PAC Person to the conclusion that the Spiritual Being which you undoubtedly are, is separate to the physical vehicle which you utilise during incarnation. TTM is a generic term to cover a multitude of solo inner world activities. It takes practice which leads to perfection. At night, we require a period of sleep generalised at around eight hours, during which the body regenerates and *the being is free from physical world restrictions*. The TTM which you practice during waking hours, will stand as training for the introduction of night time activities.

I know that you have dreamt before, and I also understand that you may have had dreams of which you are unaware. These dreams only seem relevant if you are able to enjoy the experiences after you have awakened, even though they may also have been fun at the time they actually occurred. We have already discussed that sleep is a shortened version of death ... the locations are potentially the same, just as are the possibilities for experience; general mental universe activities, knowledge and self realisation are all possible during sleep time; and perhaps more important is the accessibility of spiritual enlightenment, enhancement, enablement and empowerment!

Sleep is a unique time when the viewpoint which is you, can roam the astral, mental and spiritual realms, without an exhaustion of initial will power normally required during waking hours for detachment from the physical vehicle. Journeys which take a long time on the physical plane, are accomplished in the time it takes to think. Things that you would like to have said to your friend at work but were too embarrassed to do so, can be said in any manner of fashions. Houses can be built in an instant, businesses can boom, research is easy, meetings occur, political decisions are executed, and yes, sex may even happen between two consenting adults.

This is a huge topic which I must treat quite superficially within the context I find myself writing. Let me be clear, I am suggesting that activities which occur during sleep time can have a direct and beneficial effect on your waking hours. This is not some fancy or theory ... some of the most *respectable* people I know utilise sleep time as their most precious aspect of existence.

The sleep universe, just like the astral world and other dimensions, is occupying the exact same space you are in right now. In fact, you may like a quick exercise at this point to illustrate the existence of the etheric body, popularly thought to be that body which, in the very near future, will become visible to the naked, physical eyes of more and more of us. It sometimes helps visualisation, to utilise cartoon imagery to begin with when dealing with abstractions ...cartoon phantoms may help your visualisation of the etheric vehicle.

丸

Wherever you are right now, gently push your hand against a wall until touching. Do the same thing again, only this time, when your hand is around three inches from the surface, perceive the sensation of energy between your hand and the surface. Get aware of the energy becoming denser as your hand draws nearer to the surface. Acknowledge this energy as your aura, or etheric body. It is not dissimilar to the surrounding ethers of planet earth which may be known as the planet's aura.

Of course, the etheric body can freely move through the dense form of matter, and this may cause us to disbelieve it as an entity and physical actuality. The possibilities are for you to pursue and utilise. The point now relevant, is the fact that most of us waste sleep time, just as the less aware members of our community waste waking hours. The first exercise that you must introduce into your daily regimen, is an instruction to yourself before you go to sleep

197

each night; you may call it an inculcation ... *I will remember the events which occur whilst my body sleeps.* When you wake up, for a short while you will inhabit that cross over territory between the states of being asleep and awake. Develop a routine whereby you relive what occurred during sleep. Practice this and it will become ever easier.

This is not a quick fix of well being I am dealing in here. This subject we call continuity of consciousness, once embraced, will be with you for the rest of all time ... *eternity!* There is no limit to the possibilities, and it is this fact which sets my approach to personal development apart from the more physically oriented trick regimes.

You are now aware of the potential for conscious existence during sleep, and as you practice, you may note that unless you fall into the *exceptional category,* your will during sleep time, is not very powerful in its exertions. You may find that you drift from one experience to the next, learning little and making slow headway. Eternity awaits, do not rush and refrain from chastising any inabilities you may have experienced, and understand that it is only a question of time and experience before advancement will be forthcoming.

The next step in this ongoing exercise, is to suggest to yourself before sleep, that you wish a certain thing to happen ... *I would like to speak with my boss ... I want to fly above London ... I wish to make up with a friend ... I want to spend one million pounds ... I need to learn more about knitting, mechanics, stocks, shares, gardening, engineering, life, you and me ...* recall any happenings immediately as you awaken.

Although sex is a low physical harmonic of creation, it is a subject with which we must all deal during incarnation. The days of abstaining for spiritual gain are drawing to a close as we enter a celebratory period of *all* that is accessible to humanity. Sexual intercourse will eventually be unnecessary, as we proceed towards the Vulcan period of our incarnate existence. It was not used for procreation in the early days of etherial life on this planet, and has only become solid and compulsory for corporeal creation, as we plummeted towards the bottom of the involution spiral. As we evolve upward, our powers of creation will render such mundanaties obsolete. It is a sad person whose only expression of creation is through sex.

Sexual intercourse is not only possible in the astral world ... it is rampant! It is one of the most common elements of desire which the Silent Knights spend time dissolving through an emanation of true love and forgiveness, when such activity has become crystallised into the *astral crust* through it being out of harmony with *The Divine Plan.* It is however, a disease free activity, and two capable people are quite at liberty to engage in sexual intercourse on this plane. The physical ramifications of such relationships do not exist, and of course the temptation for multiple partners does.

You will find through practice, that all sensations are experienced by the physical body as well as the astral body. They can be weak or intense. I write about sex in this context, because some of us find that it is an extremely powerful motivating force. If it is this activity that will attract you into these inner worlds, then I see no reason to dissuade you from engaging sex in this manner.

Let me be quite clear however, in the fact that it is an extremely base, lower plane activity, which will get you nowhere except those places which I wish you to know ... the inner worlds! Make sure that this activity does not become a fixation, and may I leave you in no doubt that the other person with whom you have any such relationships, is aware of them, to a greater or lesser extent, just as you are. I may also add that you will only find those people in such places, of a disposition similar to yourself, so if this is not your aspiration, treat this level only as a springboard. The degree and quality of physical manifestation on the astral plane, is usually related to the quality of the human beings involved.

It is during sleep, when you will find a far more beneficial activity available to you, for the inner worlds are frequented by spiritual teachers usually performing a service on a lower plane to which they are karmically entitled. *Night Schools* are the establishments created by such people, and if you are aware of such actualities, then that is the first step towards you coming into contact with them. There are as you may gather, many varying levels of instruction available, and you will be helped into the most beneficial situation for the process in which you are living at the time. I understand that there are also tables for those still insisting on the consumption of alcohol before sleep; a habit which I understand can be detrimental to night studies.

The idea which we must encourage, is the retention of all teachings for utilisation during the waking state. We must constantly work at an alignment of spirit, mind and body, all the while drawing down to the lowest aspects of ourselves, as many of the higher qualities that are available. In Premier State, the Spiritual Being which you are, is all knowing. In the original Premier State, this all knowing amounted to *being*. Through form, we gather *in-form-ation*, and it is this information which we can cherish and carry back with us to our reunion, which will take the shape of an *informed* Premier State.

Night classes are but one possibility available to you whilst asleep, but for the time being, I feel the most important. Practice the retention of data, and work at ever clearer and brighter awareness during sleep periods. This astral activity can be dark as well as light, and, just as you are responsible for your own karma, so are you the only one able to judge the merits of any action you may wish to engage yourself with. If you decide to meet a business acquaintance who is less able than yourself operating in this inner world, and then consequently find yourselves engaged in negotiations, you must decide on an operating basis and the limits to your powers of persuasion. You may find your boss and plant subconsciously into his thoughts, ideas to increase your salary. This is obvious and dark. You cannot ever use abilities you find yourself with that others may not have, for purely selfish ends. I will say no more, lest this volume become a book of warnings!

Ramana Maharshi, the alleged *Last of the Great Living Saints,* said that the state of self realisation was like being awake during sleep! I encourage you to explore all possibilities, during these time periods which may amount to one third of each incarnation. It is a mark of true personal development to embrace all information that is new to you with a freshness of mind and a faith ever strong.

Interdependence

If this is not a natural tendency, then it is one which must be nurtured. It is a way of the future and as a microcosm, we should emulate the great macrocosm of *The One Life.* This means working with people. Both *the PAC* and my *PeRFECT WORDS and MUSIC Limited* business, have policies of interdependence, yet we have succeeded in establishing such rapport with others, but few times.

There is a personal development company also verbally espousing this philosophy, who summoned me for a meeting and promptly offered me a job ... under the guise of interdependence. They wanted control, and this is not interdependence! It is a much maligned, misused and mangled phrase, yet I persevere with it in the full knowledge that it will become increasingly obvious to more and more people as time progresses, that it is indeed the only way forward.

Interdependence is a blending of skills that the alchemists of old would have been justly proud of. Advanced PAC Practitioners know their own capabilities and understand that it is through mixing, matching, combining, and fusing, that harmony is achieved through progress. Interdependence is an understanding of the differing inherent qualities in each of us, often through the dominant ray qualities currently exhibiting in our lives, and thus, *assertive qualities do not overpower the more mystical attributes which may be ours ... loving feelings are not doused by the pragmatic ... creation is not controlled by the status quo.*

Interdependence is an acknowledgement of what naturally exists within each of us ... without the desire to instigate change in another for what we consider to be a more important *way of being.* The actions of a Silent Knight in the flowing of love and forgiveness, are thus interdepending with emanations of what are considered to be a less desirable nature ... if our concepts of what is good and bad are in agreement!

Interdependence is living by example, and not forcing change through coercion; change is what we all must do constantly. Following the great macrocosmic example, there is nothing quite so certain as the fact that every single thing in existence must at some point in time *start,* and then *stop.* The action in between we call *transformation!* We now have a useful equation which can be added to the modus operandi which will power our mission statement from guide five ...

Start ... Transform ... Stop

You may think that such a statement is obvious and not worthy of page space, yet you would be much mistaken. If you know that this cycle of action is inevitable, then you can manipulate events to suit your particular time scale. Thus, a point from the visualisation section of your mission tool may state ... *I enlarge my circle of friends* ... you may be three years into the full operation of your

202

mission before instigating such action, yet when you do, knowledge of the *Start Transform Stop* equation, or STS, will ensure a balance. You will begin, the list will alter, your tastes will change, people will come and go, then you must stop additions unless your circle of friends are to become a group of acquaintances.

Every cycle of action, *from a galaxy to a human life to the painting of a house,* will STS ... know the formula and you will find as the months drift by, that you have enriched your power base through this knowledge. When you interdepend, STS the aspects of the relationship, and you can make it last forever!

Pressing the right buttons

A switch exists inside of you, which can transform your whole life if you can only find it, and then learn how to get it into the *on* position. You see, this switch can be any number of similar variations to those which we use in the physical universe. *A rocker switch, an on-off button, a slide, a cord, a contact breaker point, remote control,* along with the many other variations, are all types of on-off devices which we utilise for the purpose of control.

You can live without ever touching your device, yet you may know without any doubt that those people you utilise as examples of excellence, have all knowingly or unknowingly found this switch and enabled it. The genius has this button in the *on* position, and very often is also in a state of cosmic consciousness. The involutionary process which I have already described and aligned with personality, gave us a state of *self consciousness.* The evolutionary process we are now engaged with, which I have aligned to character, will give us all *cosmic consciousness.*

Many well known historical figures throughout the ages have possessed this trait in advance of the masses, and most will be known to you. The obvious examples are *perhaps,* Galileo and

Pythagoras; but most certainly Buddha, Christ, St Paul, Mohammed, Plato, Dante, William Blake and Walt Whitman. William Shakespeare, *or was it Francis Bacon,* and Charles Dickens demonstrated through their very observations of life, that *a degree* of cosmic consciousness had to be present. Alice Bailey, Madame Blavatsky, Bishop Leadbeater, Max Heindel, Annie Besant, Henry Thomas Hamblin, Yogi Ramacharaka and a host of others engaged in the dissemination of Ageless Wisdom must also have degrees of cosmic consciousness. Abraham Lincoln was thought to be aware in this manner, as was Thomas Edison. Can you see that cosmic consciousness will always be advantageous, and it is an awareness that can be cultivated!

The switch you seek will only enable the success mechanism if you can get it to the *on* position; the switch I urge you to find however, has a dual function, for it both enables physical success, and guarantees spiritual fulfillment. It is marked *Cosmic Consciousness,* and printed beneath is a warning ... *do not touch unless you wish your whole outlook to be transformed!*

My first book, *You Can Always Get What You Want,* guided your finger onto the button which enabled you to obtain this lifetime success of a material nature, with an eye to the real you. My second book, *Before the Beginning is a Thought,* steered you towards the mental universe involving thought creation of a cyclical nature in line with the seasons. This third book which I call *Empowerment,* is an introduction to cosmic consciousness and it completes *the Body, Mind, Spirit trilogy.* These three books are not even the tip of an iceberg, which metaphorically describes the amount of enlightenment available elsewhere.

You will have already noted down some titles of other books which I have so far recommended, and you will also see that a bibliography exists towards the end of this book, as a guide to further stimulating reading and listening. I make a point of not ever paying for guidance in the ageless wisdom, and make contributions to individuals and organisations only when I see fit. I align myself with no particular group of teachings, yet embrace them all. I stay clear of many so called new age do's and don'ts that are not real to me, and I am sure that by this point in the book you understand that burning joss sticks and wearing patchouli oil does not culminate in spiritual attainment!

The last thing we need in our quest for spiritual awareness is another sect or cult!

Such organisations have wreaked havoc with peoples faith, as have the established churches for many of us who found nothing spiritual of any description within their portals. God is in you, and you take your church wherever you go. Share your positivity with others and spread happiness. You do not need any external stimuli for this to occur. The Positive Attitude Club is a concept and a physical actuality. Advanced PAC Practitioners do not *need* to physically attend as proof of beingness! ... yet, transcendees downover *do* come along to share and experience other viewpoints.

The PAC will last as long as it is needed and I expect it to dissolve around the year 2193. Membership does not guarantee you positivity; only you can do that! Joining organisations or declaring that you are a certain way, does not always mean that you have found the button. The device I describe is a switch of magnificent proportions, and it is only great strength which will cause it to move into the enable position. There are many incremental positions along the way towards full empowerment, but I guarantee you this ... the last position for any human being is called cosmic consciousness.

Find that button and press it. The picture that will unfold as pressure on the button increases, will be a vista of beauty unobtainable without this cosmic vision I describe.

Turbo charge ... the answers within you

It is very easy to equate knowledge with achievement, yet it can only ever be part of any picture ...

Personal Development is a PAC Person with a hand on the heart and a thought in the head.

People get hooked on books, subjects, personalities, tricks, audio cassette programmes and videos. I hear evidence of this almost every day of my life ... *have you got the latest whatsisnames book ... that so and so isn't half good at putting it over ... if you want a healing go to her ... he pulled ten thousand people into Wembley ... she must be good, her videos are all over the place ...*

I have always used music business analogies to describe the world of personal development, but I find these comparisons have become more factual and less metaphorical. *The follow up single has become the follow up book ... the new album is now the latest audio cassette tape programme ... the video is still the video ... the live tour now follows all new releases,* as it always did in the music business during the days when artists were able to reproduce a reasonable resemblance to their records in City Halls around the Country.

Your personal development is not in your association with a product or a person. You do not become the embodiment of a philosophy just because you join a group called whatever ... *a Theosophist is not Theosophy ... A Rosicrucian is not Rosicrucianism ... a World Server is not the Lucis Trust ... a PAC Member is not the PAC Philosophy ... an Anthroposophist is not Anthroposophy!*

This is an important distinction for each and every one of us to make. It is only after making such distinction that you may further qualify your outlook by the observation that a *sample* of any particular group studying a specific body of knowledge *will exhibit the physical manifestation of that knowledge to a degree,* and that such people are the only visible signs of an otherwise abstract philosophy! Accordingly, you may judge the *effectiveness* of a philosophy by the impression it leaves on those who study it, and the impact these people have on others and their surroundings.

Turbo charging your future is about making very definite distinctions in your life, and the most important is the separation of yourself from whatever you belong to. You cannot ever hide behind the corporate shield and then announce yourself to be wholly responsible for all that exists around you. Just as you cannot be what you are looking at and you are not what you own, you certainly are not what you belong to!

All the answers that you will ever need for your existence are within you, and it is only external stimulus that is needed to raise the fires of knowledge that live deep down inside us all. Turbo charging your existence is the regeneration of internal energies. You may feed your intellect with knowledge and this can be very efficacious in having an apparency of being the why which you had been waiting for, yet it is never more an overlooked piece of the jigsaw.

For the game of incarnate life of course, the picture is different. You need information for business, data on relationships, the skinny on trends and the gen about gizmos. Differentiate between you and this life and it will become increasingly easy to develop turbo power for your boost towards the mission.

Rocket Fuel
Now that you know about the art of differentiation, I advise you to begin your survey of the market place. It is here that you will

find the myriad of philosophies which can set you on course for the stars, just as much as they can stop you in your tracks if you fill up on the wrong octane. As with everything, the pure always has lower harmonics that are not so pristine, as well as downright fakes, and so it is in the world of personal development.

There are three types of work available for your perusal ... *observational, conversational and inspirational!* All have their place on the Path, but yet again the law of correspondence means that there are always lesser aspects of every good. It is more apparent in this world of spiritual enlightenment than anywhere. Just as you have the quality broadsheet newspapers, and, the *dwell on sensational* tabloids, so we have on the increasingly present *mind, body and spirit* shelves of the mainstream bookstores, a variety of works most of which amount to no more than commercial exploitation of precious subject matter.

It is obvious that all but the exceptional publishing companies are only going to entertain mass popularity works for their lists. This is why we find so many sub standard palmistry, astrological predictions, tarot, occult black magic, new age healing and fortune telling books around. If you want this type of work then drift with the mass and support the near sighted regimes endemic in most publishing companies. Buy them only if you deserve them! Do not think for one moment that you will unlock the mysteries with such ill fitting keys. You may find the odd helpful hint and the occasional titillating titbit, but if you want the real thing then you must contact the source material.

What makes this book different is that it contains aspects of all three varieties of works available that I previously described. It is a blend that points you in the direction of higher and more important books in the bibliography, and a fusion only possible through my experiences of many different and differing philosophies; the illustrations externalise some experiences of

Dani; the end letter and occasional references tell us something of a Silent Knight. The work as a whole acknowledges source materials and does not claim total inspirational originality for its constituent parts; only the whole. As I once heard Torkom Saraydarian say on a video I had the pleasure to view about *cleansing of the heart;* when asked by a friend what he thought of the book that this friend had just written, he replied, *fine, but where are the speech marks?* Perhaps it was a reworking of public domain data, but that does not excuse an individual from acknowledgement of others!

Turbo charging allows the recycling of energies for a variety of reasons; rocket fuel is the high octane element of your propulsion which will thrust you forward at a speed which only you can slow down. I advise you to proceed with caution and honour. Remain true to your high ideals and replace those lesser paradigms with new maps of the changing terrain.

The way you see life is through your paradigms, and it must ever be born in mind that these paradigmatic mental maps through which you view your surroundings, are not the actual territory. Your viewpoint, no matter how valid, authoritative and user friendly it may be, is just that ... *your viewpoint!* For physical existence to be a particular way, it has to be agreed upon by a relevant number of viewpoints. It is for this reason, and in keeping with the Silent Knight philosophy, we must agree that the planet earth which we currently utilise as home, is a peaceful and lovingly creative environment. When enough of us have agreed that to be so, it will be!

✺

Visualise World Peace ... Together ... With Love

This kind of visualisation and utilisation of your potential is the most powerful rocket fuel in existence. It creates an environment in which you can prosper and live out your dreams. It is the ultimate *win for all formula!* If you inculcate into your beingness a desire to live by the *win for all philosophy,* you will always be ahead of the competition, who will eventually seek to emulate your habits. All other formulae for the game of life are outmoded, and it is now actually fashionable to live and do business utilising the *win for all ingredient.* Open accountancy procedures are evident between firms which conduct business together, involving great amounts of trust and interdependence. Unconditional guarantees, are now widespread; they rely on honesty for their effectiveness, and I do not know of any firms who once having deployed such a policy, have regressed into old and less trusting ways.

Maintaining momentum

There is no end to improvement! Once you have begun to explore your potential, it becomes evident that there is no turning back on the journey, once commenced. There are resting points, and the odd season here and there for a little indulgence of self gratification. The further you travel, the further you want to travel. You know more than you know you know, and as each piece of the jigsaw fits into place, the excitement it generates spurs you on towards even greater achievement ; often at a time when spirits are flagging and doubt has crept in through the back door.

A quick fix now and again is human, and such aspiration is evident in the most spiritual of us. It is only those of you who are inherently drawn towards such shallow endeavours that need ponder their significance. If the line on your graph of personal achievement is forever rising, then no matter how small the angle is from inception to current position, celebrate! You are on the road to continuous victory, and the maintenance of momentum is a pleasure.

You *will* need to study more of the ageless wisdom! If it is not pleasurable, then you are not reading the right material. This can be for a number of reasons; perhaps the philosophy you have chosen is *not the one for you!* Perhaps you are not following my rule of *gradual graduation* and you have delved into the deep end of a body of material which is totally unsuitable, as it cannot be understood without foundational attention of a less forceful, but equally relevant nature. This is most often the case. Everyone wants the conclusion yesterday and that, I am afraid, is a quick fix which cannot be served up to you in this particular department of life.

As you maintain momentum, it is wise to bear in mind that true achievers rarely brag about their success. This can be infuriating if you wish to know about a certain aspect of a particular something, as people will rarely tell of their subjective experiences. *Avatar for hire ... let me tell your future ... Guru lives here ... it's all in the cards ... I am in touch with the Masters ... I was Napoleon in a previous life ... Beethoven writes through me ...* are all examples of danger signs. Yet, it must be made clear that all such statements are possible. It is the clever and worldly Advanced PAC Practitioner who avoids cynicism when dealing with potentially fraudulent claims of a spiritual nature. Remember that only one being was a particular Napoleon ... and has not Beethoven picked up a new body by now?

Someone I know, during a particular mutual membership into the beliefs of a certain philosophy which utilised incidents from past lives to help cure present psychosomatic dispositions, listened to five different people in one day talk about their past lives as Jesus Christ. At least four of them were suffering from ID Adoption and I have enough spiritual intuition to state quite categorically that the fifth was also dreaming. It is a human failing to adopt what is considered to be the winning identity. It is not part of the power formula however! Learn to be yourself, and there are few inculcations more powerful than the simple repetition of **I Am.** If you ponder the words as a spirit, mind and body, this mantram

211

will truly identify you as the only real I which you are.

Let me acknowledge that you are and I am; forever the two of us remain ... together ... living *The One Life* in which we are outposts of consciousness for the greater whole, and a single viewpoint of the many. We are the universe which has been created by us all, and the aspirations that we live with today are the accomplishments of tomorrow. Think the highest and most honourable thoughts you are capable of manifesting in your inner world of mind, for it is these contemplations that mould tomorrow's world.

You are a special person and that quality will remain with you forever. The Path leading to ever increasing amounts of awareness is steep if you wish, and long if you want. It is whatever you desire it to be. Personal Development lasts more than a lifetime, and the truly far sighted of us all, are the students of greater teachings who build this lifetime as a platform for the next. You will begin the next cycle elevated by the accomplishments of this one.

You are now empowered!

a silent knight

Dear Phil,

You have asked me to elucidate the nature of my current spiritual activities and I am now in a position to do so; I am a *Silent Knight.* This newly coined phrase will hold an assortment of disparate connotations to a variety of people, and will impinge on their personalities in many differing ways. So, I am forced to involve myself in this plane of personalities while defining the term precisely for the benefit of all.

I will use analogies and examples that most of us understand in this material world, and in so doing I will endeavor to explain something of the non material planes, which are for the purposes of this letter, the etheric, astral, and mental worlds. Please understand that they are only analogies, and cannot be scrutinised or extrapolated too deeply, or they will confuse the issue.

The precise definition of a *Silent Knight* is ... *One who at the very least, thinks of the words, LOVE and FORGIVENESS.*

That is the pure and simple definition. Nothing more and nothing less. Defining in this fashion is of course, like Einstein putting his theory of relativity in the simple equation, $e=mc2$. If he had stopped there, few if any of us, would have much understanding of what he had been trying to impart. My intention is to share understanding so I shall explain further!

First of all, in giving out this information, I am immediately disqualifying myself from membership within the hushed ranks of *Silent Knights,* since the expanded clarification of the term includes the activities, attitudes, and responsibilities of *Silent Knights;* the first qualification states that *such a person does not indicate to anyone that he or she is a Silent Knight.* This is why I have asked you to keep my name anonymous, and trust that you will. You know of my activities through necessity, and I am effective in this state of sustained anonymity.

Just in case you or anyone else mistakenly take this as some type of an ego trip for me to gain status as a groovy mystic, may I explain that there is very solid arcane reason for such silence, which I will mention several times I am sure. It is also the reason why Masters of the Wisdom, for the most part, rarely reveal themselves. It involves them cruelly and unnecessarily in the material plane, where challenges of the games between personalities are played over and over again, emphasizing separateness and conflict. If we are to evolve upward by seeking higher consciousness levels, we must remove our constant attention from that aspect of life.

How?

Through meditation, contemplation, concentration and anonymity, which includes the concept of silence; subjects in themselves which I am sure are familiar to you. *Silence is the only utterance we make that cannot be misquoted* ... a concept I know of which you are aware!

So, here we go ... I am just going to let it flow as it comes to me, and I am hoping that help from the higher planes will get this powerful and needed activity spread as widely and as rapidly as possible.

Why *Silent Knight?* I admit that I am using the mundane, public relations type method of getting attention in using *buzz words* or *catch phrases;* not for ego purposes, but as an attempt to stimulate curiosity in the activity.

Curiosity stimulates attention!

As I will later illustrate, there is a cosmic crisis occurring, for which we need the attention of millions, perhaps even billions, of fellow human beings! A coined word or phrase once defined, understood and accepted, becomes a *thought package,* which saves us the arduous task of going through all the details of a particular concept time and again whenever the subject is embraced. You can think of many such words or phrases which we use every day. *Silent* needs no explanation, but *Knight,* may not be so obvious.
Some dictionary definitions which are to hand, describe such a person as follows ... *a medieval gentleman-soldier, usually of high birth, raised by a sovereign to privileged military status after training as a page or squire, and; a defender or champion, or zealous upholder of*

216

a cause or principle, also; the devoted champion of a lady."

I have not included all definitions of which I am aware ... only those that come close to the significance of what we are trying to do. Anything describing status is immediately not applicable, so references to high birth and privileges should be ignored. The substance we are looking for falls into the description of behavior and qualities befitting a knight; ***chivalry!*** That *is* an appropriate term. *A Silent Knight is a chivalrous person who remains, to the best of his ability, silent about it.* The play on words will also be a relevant aspect, as it mentally associates with the song *Silent Night.*

This may remind us of The One who practiced, through His living and dying example, *LOVE AND FORGIVENESS.* There is much more to be said on this point but let it stand for now.

We are talking here about individual souls rather than personalities, when using any reference to *Silent Knights.* Let me explain further. There is a book, which coincidentally to the acronym for your Positive Attitude Club, uses in its title the abbreviation PAC, signifying Parent, Adult and Child. This was the author's coined names for the three states of mind we demonstrate in our everyday living. I would like to stop there, but on reflection will not leave you hanging. It is as though we move the body through different rooms in a house, when we as souls, move our attention from one emotional room or state, to another. Depending on conditions, we seem to behave sometimes as a child ... *I'll scream if I don't get it!* ... a parent ... *isn't it terrible!* ... or an adult ... *please pass the salt.* If we were not on automatic pilot most of the time, we could actually take on any one of the PAC states at will ... just mock it up mentally with imagination, and run up and down an imaginary emotional tone scale.

I prefer the idea of *wearing a hat,* to describe a particular role, which I believe originated on the old American railroads. We wear different hats all the time figuratively speaking. In the office your hat is as a boss? ... a secretary? ... whatever it may be. You go home and you are a husband? ... mother? ... grandparent?

How does this information connect? Well, a person is a *Silent Knight* when he wears that hat, or perhaps *helmet and visor* is more appropriate!. It can occur at any time; perhaps when reading, saying, thinking, or directing attention to the concepts of *LOVE AND FORGIVENESS*. You were a *Silent Knight* just then as you read those words. Only while you have your attention on those two words are you a *Silent Knight*.

Maybe you will involve yourself for a matter of seconds. You could be a *Silent Knight* for hours, days, months or even years. Our abilities as well as interests vary widely, and many varieties and time periods of service will evolve along the lines of this principle.

What good is all this that I describe so enthusiastically? I am hoping to make it worth more than the time it will take you to read my words. The problem is that when we are trying to transfer an idea or understanding from ourselves to another, we have to use one word at a time ... serial communication, as on a computer modem. Each word might *key-in* a different meaning and the idea may get lost. How great it would be if we could pass on a concept as a rubber stamp, or as Robert Monroe calls it on the mental plane, *a rote;* we would cease being so impatient and confused.

May I use another analogy ...

Think for a minute about the supply of oxygen in the world. Thank God it is so huge and plentiful, but surely you must know that it is not unlimited. There are tremendously huge amounts of it being gobbled up every day in forest fires, volcanoes, jet engines, breathing life, and so it goes on. If oxygen were not being replaced in the same huge amounts every day, we would have died out as a race, long ago. Where is it coming from? Well, of course we all know that plants recycle our carbon dioxide into oxygen, but stop and think again ... it emerges *ONE MOLECULE,* or, *ONE BUBBLE AT A TIME!* ... from the jillions of plants over the earth! As an aside, I read somewhere that the algae in the sea, and sea plants, are responsible for the greater amounts of oxygen replacement in the atmosphere.

And now for the analogy ... Love and Forgiveness are words, and therefore they create or evoke thought forms. This is our most common way of producing a thought form..... through the use of words. That is why our language is of no barrier in locking in on the thought forms of

218

the Chinese, Japanese, French ... whoever. Their words for the same things produce the same or similar thought forms. The more people who put their attention on these two words, Love and Forgiveness, the more mental energy is pu' into those thought forms, which makes the effect much bigger and duration in the nether planes longer. Unfortunately, this is exactly what is being done by most humans right now, with their attention predominantly on the negative and destructive thought forms constantly hammering at them through the media. As I will attempt to illustrate later, there is an urgent need ... an appeal ... a clarion call ... right now, for as many humans to think on these two words as is possible. **ONLY HUMAN BEINGS NEED *APPLY* FOR THE JOB, AS ONLY HUMAN BEINGS CAN *DO* THE JOB!** We are the only species that can even understand that there is a crisis.

There are megaquadrillions of thought forms abounding in the place where physical things, our actions, are first initiated ... *before the beginning is a thought,* states another of your books, Phil. Humanity's greatest source of misery is in not understanding what we do when we harbor thoughts ... not only good, but bad as well. If we think a thought casually and attach to it little importance, it is like a vapor and disappears, or reverts back into the mind stuff reservoir, which is the basic substance of that plane. If for whatever reason we hold it mentally in place through concentration, the thought further solidifies, becomes more crystallized, and begins to resonate with other similar thought forms, thus becoming a very powerful influence over others who may be unaware of the power with which they meddle. Imagine the tremendously powerful thought forms that have been generated through the reading of books, the watching of movies and television ... there are hundreds of other sources ... and now try and tell me they have not had a powerful influence in our lives and over our behavior. Violence, sex abuse and social diseases are just some of the problem effects that have been forthcoming from these sources.

The Silent Knight is addressing the cosmic problem of the now overpowering amount of negative thought forms prevailing. The good guys who very sincerely and honestly want to establish peace and goodwill toward men and women, are attempting to better things the only way they know how, with new laws, prisons, more police and rehabilitation. They should not be judged harshly *for they know not what they do.* Esoteric knowledge teaches that fighting against something evil gives it life and maintains the thought form, thus creating mental mass. This is the essence of Christ's *turning the other cheek message.* Or we can say, let it pass through without engaging, or, giving life to it.

An SK may or may not know what he is doing metaphysically and cognisance of this fact is of lesser importance to the result, even though he would accomplish more if he would expand his knowledge and understanding in this area. Which brings me to something I want stress while it is on my mind.

Who can be a Silent Knight? Can a criminal, a rapist or a serial killer? Yes! Any human being who can say, think, read or hear the words LOVE AND FORGIVENESS is being, at that moment a Silent Knight, and producing bubbles of L and F into the mental realm. Of course it is highly unlikely that the destructively negative persons used above to test the SK definition would respond to the call now being made; but if one should be touched to do so, he can send L and F just as well as anyone, and I emphasize that we do not qualify the source.

This subject is so immense, and I do wonder if I am up to the task of dissemination? Why LOVE and FORGIVENESS? God has a plan for this universe and more specifically for this planet. The plan is perfect. He needs workers for the accomplishment of the plan, and for millions of years things were going along peacefully and harmoniously. Part of the plan focussed heavily on the form of life known as humanity, and the evolution of this form, as well as others, into higher and higher consciousness and awareness. It was axiomatic that this form should have free will to experiment and do whatever it wanted. This is the Garden of Eden and Paradise of the Bible. Well, we all know what happened. We ate the forbidden fruit. Personalities developed, strong wills; dictators and emperors abounded; throughout hundreds of thousands of years these violent thought forms were constantly being held in the mental planes and grew stronger as more bodies swelled the population and gave their mental support to the negative crystals of disharmony, as they are called. We are like the moon probe in a sense. We receive energy, qualify it with experience, and relay it back to source, *and all is well at NASA.* However, if the probe behaves disharmoniously and malfunctions with its design or

220

plan, the result is a break in communication which crystallizes into problems ... disharmony.

The sad part of it is, that many Masters were sent through the ages to teach the wisdom ... or lack of it ... in what we humans were doing, but *little man* was so fascinated, and having so much fun with earthly games, he was not interested in the least about what he was doing to the astral plane. We have the same disinterest of the masses about the rain forests, ozone hole, water supply and pollution. Almost without exception, these wise beings were ridiculed and even murdered ... even he who achieved what we call Christ Consciousness, the man, Jesus of Nazareth. My understanding is that others have reached this state in other areas of the world, and they are now all as spirits, called *Elder Brothers, Ascended Masters, Brothers in Light* or perhaps *The Spiritual Hierarchy,* and all are still working to raise us from the mud. With the fantastically spiraling numbers of the world population, combined with the dwindling natural resources, and the powerful negative mental forces in thought forms becoming more and more prevalent, the extinction of life as we know it is no longer just a scary impossibility!

As we follow world events, we instinctively feel that we are being witnesses to a *world* crisis, whereas in the past we have, at best, only been concerned with *national* crises. There are already untold millions trying to remedy the situation by medium of the mental plane in the form of prayer and meditation in both private and group formations, so I am not speaking of any new or original activity ... perhaps a new division or battalion. These groups *are* getting results! ... the Berlin Wall, the fall of Russian Communism, the Arab Israeli pacts, and now Northern Ireland and England, to mention only a few examples. Sadly though, much, much, more is needed to be done and time is limited ... a state of urgency exists for this planet's rebirth. I will briefly explain ...

The Aquarian Age has dawned, with radiations from the Creator which we have not had before. Even scientists acknowledge an unknown *ray* beaming in on earth at this time. Esotericists say it is the *Golden Ray of Christ Consciousness* heralding the new Aquarian Age, which will accompany the rebirth of our planet. This will not happen without tremendous earth changes which will cause earthquakes,

221

floods, and, mass extinctions, on which I do not want to dwell for explaining our purposes. The violence of the change can be diminished somewhat if the force in the chaotic, psychic astral plane is transmuted.

WE CAN MAKE THE EARTH CHANGE LESS CHAOTIC!

What causes chaos in the psychic astral plane? It is quite simple. Man is the only generator of it, when he acts or thinks any thought forms that are out of harmony with the Great Divine and Perfect Plan of God. Out of harmony means that these thought forms vibrate at such a lower rate, they are not *tuned in* on the *God Station's* frequency, and so they cannot leave this realm to be received; thus they become *earth-bound* ... refer to my preceding NASA Probe analogy.

This *disharmony* causes a crystallization of negative *thought matter* that becomes a *cloud,* so to speak, around the earth. This exactly, *is* the *Veil of Illusion* ... *Maya* ... that is mentioned in the Eastern Wisdom Teachings, and is the *Tunnel of Darkness* experienced by those having near death experiences or NDE's. Over millions of years this has now become so dense that the Golden Ray has difficulty in bringing about the earth's rebirth, so it has to *blast* its way through, *metaphorically speaking,* to get the evolutionary task under way, and this *WILL* occur on schedule. If the cloud of disharmony is melted, transmuted, or banished, then the Ray will be able to bring in the New Age with much less violence than otherwise may be the case. You understand esoteric teachings of the Great Work, Phil. The Great Work right now is to restore *The Perfect Plan of the Creator.* There are many ways to do this. My calling is to be a Silent Knight working to dissipate the thick crust of disharmony. Humanity put it there and only we can remove it.

We are the Ground Crew!

We humans are the *only* ones who can make the positive thought forms of LOVE and FORGIVENESS, which can clear out that pollution of disharmony.

Now here is the answer to *why Love and Forgiveness?* Love is not only the most powerful force on the mental planes, it is the harmonizing force of the universe. It can bring active beings into the good life of peace and abundance ... *on Earth as it is in Heaven* ... what we all really hope for in our deepest selves. Forgiveness is an aspect of love that now needs to be radiated, broadcasted and specifically evoked into the space around the earth. It is the only means we have at our disposal for the dispellation of this disharmonious crust. It matters not who put it there, karma is not on the current agenda for discussion, you could make a good bet that each of us has done our share of contributing throughout the ages however.

Forgiveness is our lower harmonic of the *LAW of ALLOWANCES,* which you know is applicable without exception on the very high planes of *Light Beings, Elder Brothers, Ascended Masters* ... they are called by many names as I have mentioned. With much meditation and contemplation on the data I received from Patricia Diane Cota-Robles, along with the immense amount of data from my thirty and more years of metaphysical studies with meditation, I now see better exactly what is occurring in the cosmos on the higher planes, and do not argue with it as much as I used to. *Maybe I am advancing after all!*

So to try to pull together what I have said so far ... you now know about the crisis ... you know that we are called to help ... and you know that there are many already helping in the way that they know best. I offer your readers this very simple way in which *anyone* can help ... and I mean *anyone!* You do not need to go into any arduous purification rites, rituals, fasting, self denial, prayer or salaams to the east ... just as you will not receive fame for your donations ... there is no promise of salvation ... no money to be made ... no certificate ... no special disciplines or training. This may be a new dispensation in the same category as the Good News Gospel of the New Testament, with this significant difference ... we are aiming to save the *planet* and work in harmony with God's Perfect Plan, instead of trying to save *ourselves*. We are evolving from individual competition to group co-operation. Silent Knights could be considered as a special category of the *new group of world servers* described in the writings of Alice Bailey.

The Silent Knight can be the lowest form of human, yet still be working alongside the Masters right now, by simply thinking about LOVE and FORGIVENESS! What do you think will happen inside such people if they do *too much* of this service?

Phil, I am excited about this task ... anyone can work shoulder to shoulder with the Angels! I have likened it to what happens when disaster strikes; a breaking dike or an earthquake for example ... something inside of us bursts out in the form of compassion and unconditional desire to help. It may be dark along the dike and we may not know the identity of the person who fills the sand bags alongside us ... it makes no difference if he is a child abuser, rapist, priest or politician ... the help is gladly and unconditionally accepted.

Some notes of potential interest to your readers ...
1. We volunteered aeons ago from all over the universe and distant galaxies to come and help with the Aquarian Age rebirth of this planet, but if we came with full remembrance of who we really are, we would have said, *yuk,* and left early on ... so we *allowed* a veil of forgetfulness to be put over us, as well as a change in our DNA, forgot that we allowed it, and this situation remains until the job is done. The finish date is, I am told, *in the region of* 2012 AD, and at that time the veil of forgetfulness will be removed, along with the restoration of our original DNA. Then we will remember who we are and will be free to return home! *Theena and Avalon* come to mind as I write these words.

2. The golden and violet rays are coming in to change the planet's vibrations. The rays are too high in frequency for the Earth, and only we human beings can act as transformers to step down the frequency for the earth to benefit. This is being done by other world workers in so called *Earth Healing Meditations.* These are the frequencies of light ... *for knowledge, information and understanding* ... together with love ... *for harmony, peace and beauty.* Those who choose Light and Love at this time are the *Family of Light* and are another group of world workers, also called Light Workers. You must know that any of us can do a selection of many things alongside our Silent Knight dedication.

3. I was astonished when reading some of the Lucis Trust pamphlets quoting Alice Bailey and The Tibetan, to discover that I happen to be on target with the group meditations and group co creation they also emphasise. The accent I noted during our recent and mutual Lucis

224

Trust Full Moon Meditation, seems to be on exoteric physical meetings of world workers, alongside dissemination of printed matter. This is definitely needed and requires much more dedication and self sacrifice than that demanded of a Silent Knight We only differ in how a group can be defined and the simplicity of application. There is no need for meetings, rules, fees and publications. A group can simply be people who have a common interest or viewpoint. Examples could be vegetarians, golfers and artists. They can get together physically, but they usually will not; nor do they need to in order to be called a group. Since an SK is working telepathically, there is no real need to physically assemble. In fact it would destroy the silence aspect of the silent in Silent Knight. I get the feeling that this activity could be an entrance door to the inner worlds you speak of in this book, for many who have absolutely no awareness of any esoteric knowledge. If they play with L and F too much they are going to want MORE! Hooked! Gotcha! Dare we have T-shirts and bumper stickers that say **LTBLAF,** tickling the attention until it has to be asked ... *what on earth does LTBLAF mean?* Then we get to say *Let there be Love and Forgiveness!* A few more metaphorical bubbles eh?

4. An analogy of how thought forms are made active by thinking about them, could be compared to going into a dark basement where objects are stored. In the dark we see nothing there at all, but turn on a flashlight and aim it around and we see, bit by bit exactly what is in that area. We bring the object into our awareness, and give it life in our thoughts. Our *attention* behaves on thought forms like the flash light in the dark basement.

5. Another analogy, for those mechanical minded people who have trouble with visualizations that *don't look right* sometimes, which certainly happens with me ... when we are supposed to mock up a shaft of light or a ray, coming from the heart of God for instance, straight through us to the center of the earth, most people just do it ... no problem. But I asked myself, suppose someone in China was doing the same thing at the same time, I would expect two rays coming into the earth from the heart of *God from opposite directions.* Is God in two or more places? This is, of course, the confusion of our materially oriented minds thinking about conditions on the higher planes. I had to contemplate this until I conceived of an analogy that allowed me to let go of the issue.

All things material and astral, as well as mental and spiritual, float in a sea of god- stuff, like bubbles in a glass of soda water. This god-stuff is infinite *potentials;* that means everything that has ever existed, exists, and will ever exist in thought, action, and being, is present in the form of potentials.

This has also been stated in Quantum Mechanics as the vacuum, or, zero point energy ... *referring to absolute zero temperature* ... and the ether, which is not the same definition as that used in Metaphysics. All those tiny elements of matter researched in Particle Physics seeming to appear from nowhere, are therefore postulated as coming from the vacuum which fills space and is only full of *potentials.* Not being a physicist I may be in error on the details; if that is so forgive me, for I am only trying to relate some of this information to the subject we are discussing.

All things are possible with God ... except usurping the free will of His human children. A light bulb has only the potential of light until it is turned on. So this sea of god-stuff behaves like a pressure in space. Now anyone who understands liquid pressure knows that this pressure is equal on all surfaces perpendicular to the surface. If we invoke a ray of light to enter us on one side of the bubble earth, we turn on the potential in the sea, which behaves like a liquid pressure, and the ray comes in vertically no matter where we are on the bubble earth. I know that artists and poets would never need this type of mechanical description, but it sure solved a problem for me and I had to write it down to get it off my mind, and in the hope that it would help some other like minded being. It is one of the things that has come to me in my meditations this past year.

6. There is a physical condition over Los Angeles that makes a good analogy for the psychic astral crust or smog created about the earth by the acts of humans that are disharmonious with God's Perfect Plan. Los Angeles, according to actual meteorological data, has the strongest temperature inversion in the World. To those who don't know what an inversion is, I will explain. We all know that hot air rises. The reason it rises is that it is less dense that the cold air surrounding it. Therefore the heavier cold air slides under it so to speak, and pushes the hot air upward. This is well and good, but suppose the air rises until it hits a layer that is hotter? It is now the cooler air and will rise no farther.

The cold air of the Pacific Ocean lays over LA practically all the time, but there is a desert behind the mountains to the west which supplies very hot air, sometimes 120-140 degrees fahrenheit when blowing over the mountains, which is almost constantly! This creates an actual ceiling which can be seen as you rise in an airplane; the smog getting denser until there is practically no visibility at all. At its darkest, one then emerges into the brilliant light and clear visibility of clean desert air. Now this is only an analogy for the purpose of understanding the *smog of disharmony.*

7. I feel I have to inject into all this a joke we used when I sang in a Barbershop Quartet. We are admonished by the Elder Brothers in Light to keep our sense of humor ... one can get too heavy and serious in this field of Esotericism. During the rendition of a song, our tenor, who enjoyed playing the part of an idiot, would start making weird gyrations with his arms, and jerks with his body, until, with good timing, *the most important aspect of humor,* it was my job to stop the song and angrily ask him what he was doing. His reply, given with a smile ... *keeping the elephants away!* I would respond loudly and most irritably, *but there AREN'T any elephants HERE!* Very hurt, he would close the sketch with ... *well the least you could do is thank me for the good job I'm doing.*

An SK could appear to be as ridiculous as our tenor acted. But those who are cognizant of the Ageless Wisdom and Esotericism, would say that our tenor could very well be keeping the *thought forms* of elephants away. This, an SK does by simply moving awareness from the room of the material world, to the attic of the astral realms, by concentrating on Love and Forgiveness. Remember that anyone can do this, and thereby be a Silent Knight!

8. Another mechanical explanation ... somehow I feel that there is a need for such metaphysical trivia. Did you ever stop to ponder the reason why we need a body? Suppose all we had was a head for our awareness and perceptions, with an individual face for identification. Also, suppose that we did not need legs to move us around ... we could just think ourselves around ... *no gravity* ... and the same with arms ... just absorb what we want ... suppose this head ran on light and not food energy. All we would need is the head. Well, according to my studies, the awareness units known as human spirits, do not even need a head!

227

When they seem to materialize, or come through on photographs, we rarely see anything but the FACE. Without that they would not be recognized. I am told that some spirits feel uncomfortable without a body and keep it mocked up anyway. Those are the ones that appear as a complete form.

9. Continuing the trivia, Michael Gordon Scallion, in line with Ageless Wisdom and being astrologically logical, says that when we want to make something a habit ... good things, we hope ... if we will but concentrate and do it, preferably at the same time each day, for 28 days, it becomes etched into our subconscious until it is a true part of our makeup and is no longer a pretense; or, as some have said about affirmations, a lie. *You have already mentioned this in the book Phil.* I reiterate this natural law here because it is relevant to anyone wishing to partake of Silent Knight activities, who finds it difficult *to get into the habit!* The Moon, in Astrology, is ruler of our subconscious mind. If one wishes to use the full power of this tool, one should begin inculcation of a desirable behavior pattern on the new moon, for anything started at the new moon, it is said, will be completed successfully.

10. I am sure you know that as we move up in our awareness level, we begin to radiate more and more brightly in the spiritual world. This develops to the degree that we are helping God, or whoever is Creator for you, with The Perfect Plan. The more we develop in Love and Light the more we join with the light family and become points of light more easily seen by the Masters. All this you know. I only mention it, because I wonder about George Bush during his last campaign when he referred to thousands of points of light out there doing the right thing. Could he be into Esotericism? I thought this worthy of mention.

11. Remember we were talking about astrosomes and egregors recently Phil? Astrosome is Mauni Sadhu's name for the etheric body of the individual. Egregor is his name for the same type of body that forms around a group who think about the same things, whether it be a church, corporation, family, or whatever other type of group. The greater the number of people and amount of mental activity on their common field of agreement, the bigger and stronger does the Egregor become. I mention this only because it is these Egregors around the

228

groups of world servers which is the focus of our attempt at getting more and more humans into the Great Work of restoring God's Plan ... which is Perfect. I saw something appropriate to all this on a billboard ... *If we all do a little, we can all do a lot!* Remember, we humans are the only species on earth that have been given the power of Creative Visualization allowing us to get the cleanup job done. The *Egregor* of the Earth *is* the chaotic psychic astral plane. Egregors have life and intelligence as do Astrosomes, on the astral plane, and interact with us humans. Where is Satan? You got it ... he *is* that crystallized cloud of disharmony that WE HUMANS CREATED!

Loosh, according to Robert Monroe is an energy emanated from life forms when under tremendous emotional stress ... fear, pain, suffering, torturous death, and even to a lesser extent tremendous joy. This energy is as vital to some non-material beings unknown to us, as air and food is to life here on earth. There is a lot here to ponder and I must be brief ... could such Beings be considered the cosmic counterparts of the Repressives you refer to in Guide Three?

12. I want to expand on what I was saying about *who can be a Silent Knight?* Suppose you are an invalid ... bed-ridden for instance, or someone living in a Home for the Elderly and you feel more or less useless or bored, or, you are any one of the thousands, maybe millions of people in this whole world who find personal communication uncomfortable; even the starving people in some struggling African countries, or the persecuted in prisons; those with AIDS and Leprosy ... *Great God in Heaven* ... can you see what a galactic effect we could create by reaching all these people and getting across to them the Silent Knight idea, and how the use of their minds is urgently needed right now! Somehow, I think the PAC has been called on to do this. Your work is really cut out for you, Phil.

13. I have defined the Silent Knight philosophy as simply as I can ... no frills, no if's, and's, or but's, as they say. We will gladly accept a mere two second thought ... *a bubble or two* ... if that is all one wants to contribute ... and great thanks will be forthcoming for it. If the SK would like to enhance his output, here are offered suggestions which may help without getting into complicated rules, must do's, must don't's; these are strictly options to be used or ignored according to choice made by the individual SK.

229

a) You can broaden and strengthen the effect of your thinking in general by flowing Love and Forgiveness; of course, and by doing it for longer periods of time in addition to doing it more often, the inner strength multiplies accordingly. If you are sitting in the doctor's waiting room ... waiting on a plane or an elevator ... *just think of L and F.* We all have literally thousands of moments when we are, more or less mentally doing nothing. If we only knew what tremendous effect we could cause on the goal of bringing *on earth as it is in heaven* to a reality, by using those moments as an SK!

b) You can add Creative Visualization, the one *God like Power* you have that is only dimly developing in the animal kingdom, by imagining L and F in the form of a spray, or pink bubbles that have a magic perfume that spell binds people all over the world to live harmoniously, lovingly, and with tolerance of other peoples' faults. This is only an example. You can use a hose, airplanes dropping leaflets, love bugs that bite ... whatever is real to you. Mock it up. The forgiveness, you can imagine as a blow torch melting and evaporating the dirty astral crust ... or use an air hammer to break it up, spray an acid to eat it up. Again, use your imagination ... imaging ... to do it your way. You are now working, in your own way, shoulder to shoulder with the Masters! Can you possibly believe that this activity would not affect your life for the better?

However, there is a drawback, the minute you do this for personal gain, you have eliminated yourself as an SK by the fact that your attention is no longer on the *Goal of the SK.* Nothing terrible will happen ... your help will be missed ... that's all! As has already been said, *it is more fulfilling to keep one's attention on the game rather than on the score!* The benefits come as surprises; God's Grace as it is sometimes called, known to me as serendipity.

c) If you are watching the bad news on TV or reading it in newspapers, you are locked in on those negative thought forms. This is harmless enough unless you let it upset you, thus adding the powerful force of emotion and life to the astral crust. If you then relate bad news to someone else in disgust or anger, these emotions and thoughts about it all, give more life force to those thought forms, which not only maintains them in the astral smog, but adds strength, size and mass to those thought forms. It is easy to see that this could cancel out a chunk of the LOVE and FORGIVENESS being sent out ... your own as well as others. This applies to all griping, criticism and negative thoughts in general. One may say that it is irresponsible not to be enraged at what is going on in the world, and not to try and do something about it. If you feel that way, that is your right. You can still perform the basic act of an SK by just thinking of L and F. But if one holds that opinion of irresponsibility with emotion, it will cancel out some of the SK activity, and thus becomes akin to working against oneself. Know that there are countless masses of those who are *materially* doing what they believe is *responsible action* regarding the evils, but the results are minimal compared to what can be achieved by first executing desired results on the astral planes. This of course requires more participation by an increased number of people in Positive Thinking and Attitudes. Advanced PAC Practitioners fit this bill from your Positive Attitude Club, Phil.

This is real high level stuff practiced and required by the Masters, having much if not all, to do with the Law of Allowances. I find it personally tough to do, but I am working daily at the task. *Curse not the seed for not yet being a flower.* We are all becoming, and must be patient with those who do not see yet. Listen politely with patience to our friends bemoanings, and move to positive conversation as smoothly and lovingly as we are able. You would expect similar from higher spiritual entities. I am reminded of watching mountain climbers on the television. How much trust and confidence they place in each other! The most experienced is the leading man, establishing the anchor points for the safety line that everyone below can follow. In turn the man below him has the same duty to the one below him and so forth. There is no *one up man ship* game going on. It is the epitome of what and where we all are spiritually ... we should be helping each other!

Our earth plane equivalent, *as above, so below,* to the Law of Allowance, is forgiveness. By the way there is one aspect of what the SK does that keeps him operating in the higher planes. He sends out L and F as an overall and general radiation ... *emulating the Sun that shines on all alike* ... not aimed at any individual, group or entity. Nothing says he cannot do this all he wants, but it is something other than what the SK is practicing. Aiming L and F at individuals, and excluding some who *don't deserve it,* puts the SK back into the plane

231

of personalities. Can you see how our intent can move us quickly in and out of these spiritual *rooms,* or states of consciousness?

15. I hope I have not given the impression that this group of SK s is some elite gathering that is functionally separate and cannot be combined with other PAC type activities. You can be practicing any positive thinking methods you wish, and still do a bit of SK*ing* now and then. For instance the Hare Krishna Group. They do somewhat similarly by holding the thought form all their idle time on HARE KRISHNA, and by saying it out loud constantly. Similar with the Buddhists humming the AUM. These may or may not be helping to varying degrees the immediate crisis, but this is *exoteric,* and does not target the most urgent problem of dissolving the Psychic Astral Plane. It is in the game plane of personalities and polarities inviting negative criticism and reactions from those who *know not what they do.* Apparently Masters like Jesus the Christ, have learned that the people of this world do not like perfect beings in their presence. It makes them feel less perfect and bad, so the game of self justification begins, which, as we understand from history, can get very rough. Does this make it any clearer as to why there is more accomplished result through silent and egoless meditation on the mental plane? Actually this applies to the black magician as well as the white magician. Neither makes a display of what he is doing for this very arcane reason.

I am now at the close of this epistle, and as I have read, re-read and edited this until I am really exhausted, I cannot help but feel that we are dealing with the essence of what Jesus the Christ gave His Life for. In trying to teach *The Wisdom* in those days, he had to use simple arguments and parables, which are not very stable analogies, to communicate with the simple and unenlightened souls of that era. The human problem is essentially the same now, except that today we have actually been blessed with more acceptance and understanding of all this esoteric knowledge on how the universe operates on the mental and spiritual levels. How could He have explained all this to non scientific minds? Even the last words he said, *Father, forgive them, for they know not what they do,* makes Him the greatest of all Audible Silent Knights. They knew they were killing him, so that is not what He was referring to. He saw that they literally did NOT know that they were hugely adding to the astral smog of disharmony with God s Plan,

232

and he wanted to transmute that crystallization of the horrible deed immediately with FORGIVENESS!

I have spent half of my life seeking, with little or few results regarding first hand knowledge or experience. However, I did get a great deal of second hand knowledge or data. First hand knowledge is true *knowing* ...experiencing. Second hand knowledge is very useful, but is *knowing about* ... until, by testing and using such knowledge it becomes first hand knowing. The quote you have used early in this book from Madame Blavatsky's *Isis Unveiled* is an excellent indication of some mental challenges I have personally grappled with. Patricia Diane Cota-Robles' meditation tape, in which one attains toward reaching one's higher Self ... THAT I AM and not *this I am* ... gave me some of these ideas in rudimentary form and helped synthesize previous second hand knowledge.

In these meditations she carries you to a state of quietness where you have asked THAT I AM to take charge of the four lower vehicles (Physical, Etheric Mental, and Emotional bodies) and instruct you as to what you should do in harmony with HIS Plan. Just before that, you state what you would like your life work to be. I stated I wanted to be a healer. The Mission Statement technology that you describe may have helped me had I been cognisant of it ... I tried physically healing people with little success. Maybe I am becoming an Earth-Healer!

I did this meditation daily for a month or so and I was enjoying the bliss as I always do in meditation, but was not trying to force anything: I am sure I completed at least one cycle of the moon coincidentally, and I got a clear concept of what the problem was with the astral crust and how forgiveness was the only solution ... it literally dissolves the crust, and only humans can forgive, thereby transmuting that mess. Also, an understanding came to me, that harmony with the Divine Plan needed restoring on the earth plane, and that LOVE, *the friendliest force* as you call it, is the most powerful energy to accomplish this. That, and the idea that these forces do their greatest work when transmitted, or radiated, by humans *impersonally* to the atmosphere of the whole planet. This especially appealed to me because I am not a physical group type person, and instinctively avoid such assemblies, although they definitely are necessary. Somehow I feel there are enough doing that type of work and that any good I can do is best done

233

alone and anonymously. This I have already told you.

You were reminding me how much I must know with so many studies behind me, yet I just did not feel up to the altitude you were affording me. I told you that with respect to this wisdom field I feel very humble and limited in my knowing. It was your insistence, and questioning along these lines of the Ageless Wisdom, that got me interested in the books you were studying. This awakened memories in me, of when I was first getting into the esoteric field. I then came to England and we had our fantastic talks ... free hand so to speak ... and as I began to browse through the Lucis Trust material and your Alice Bailey books, then finally at that full moon meditation in London, it all fell in place and the name Silent Knight hit me like a boulder. You got it immediately too, but I asked you to promise me that you would not put it out to the PAC until I had a chance to define it and its character, as well as the possible effects it would have. This I have done to the best of my ability. The fact that you already have established a PAC newsletter, I cannot help but feel guided to you with this, for spreading this activity to the world, because I, by myself, would not have undertaken the task of preaching this New Dispensation of the Aquarian Age. What better thing in life could happen to you, me, and the PAC, than to be instruments for relieving the stress of the psychic astral plane, obviating the necessity of much violence and destruction which at this time is destined to happen. I could literally cry with joy, yet I know such emotional reactions are far behind me! Phil, I have you to thank for pulling it out of me. You were the catalyst! I honestly felt I had nothing to offer, because it seemed to me that it has all been said before, and perhaps better than I could possibly ever have done.

Let this be our pebbles in the pond, that send the waves of Love and Forgiveness in all directions. Let us pray that somehow, billions will be touched by this simple Silent Knight Philosophy.

God Bless you and yours ...

a Silent Knight

Further Stimulating Reading and Listening
can be undertaken by obtaining the following books and audio cassette tapes programmes

Various works by _books_
Alice A Bailey

Various works by _books_
H P Blavatsky

The Kybalion Hermetic Philosophy _book_
Three Initiates

Before the Beginning is a Thought _book and cassette_
Phil Murray

You Can Always Get What You Want _book, single and multiple cassettes_
Phil Murray

Empowerment _book, single and multiple cassettes_
Phil Murray

As A Man Thinketh _book and cassette_
James Allen

Memories _cassette_
Nico Thelman

The Plan _cassette_
Nico Thelman

A Guide to the Mysteries _book_
Ina Crawford

Cosmic Consciousness _book_
Richard Maurice Bucke

The Seven Rays of Energy _book_
Michal J Eastcott

The Aquarian Gospel of Jesus The Christ _book_
Levi

The Astral Plane _book_
C W Leadbeater

Thought Power _book_
Annie Besant

Dynamic Thought _book_
Henry Thomas Hamblin

The Rosicrucian Cosmo-Conception   book
                                    Max Heindel
Gleanings of a Mystic   book
                                    Max Heindel
Christ In You   book
                        published by Watkins Bookshop
The Varieties of Religious Experience   book
                                    William James
Human Destiny   book
                                Lecomte du Noüy
Raja Yoga or Mental Development   book
                                Yogi Ramacharaka
Various works by   books and cassettes
                        Patricia Diane Cota-Robles

*Some of these products may be obtained from your local
bookstore ... most are available from the* PAC.

the **PAC**
Mission Statement
Through dissemination of quality spiritual and worldly material,
living the talk and enjoying the Path of Transformation,
we aim to render whatever assistance is required for
The Journey

Ultimate Goal
Premier State

the **PAC** philosophy
The improvement of personal life through positive attitudes, benefits
Humanity as a Whole

Visualisation Statement
A large and increasing membership
We aid members' awareness of positive reading, writing and viewing materials
We help the world, with a constant output of positive affirmations from all members
We influence the world for the better in every way possible
We show by example, that the PAC philosophy works
We influence the Media, and World Governments, with our philosophy
We exist wherever there are people who can benefit and prosper from PAC Principles
We are revered as an organisation of high principle, honour and integrity
We are available for consultation, concerning disagreements between peoples of the world, with the aim of solving all problems on a win for all basis
Happiness during the Return Journey

Phil Murray
Leader of *the* **PAC** 17 March 1995

FEELING GOOD ABOUT YOURSELF HAS A POSITIVE IMPACT
ON EVERYONE AND EVERYTHING AROUND YOU

The Positive Attitude Club

Madeira, Hunts Road, St Lawrence, Isle of Wight PO38 1XT, England

E MAIL: 101376.154@COMPUSERVE.COM

http://ourworld.compuserve.com/homepages/Phil_Murray_7

WELCOME TO THE CONSTANTLY EVOLVING PAC CONCEPT
The Positive Attitude Club accepts applications from anyone wishing
to join in with the spirit of the idea. All we ask is that they
embrace the philosophy that positive attitudes are helpful. This
is a members' organisation; direction, activities and content ideas
are always welcome. In line with our plans for the expansion of
this beautifully simple philosophy, every member is invited to begin
their own local PAC along the lines of *forward thinking through creative
discussion*. In harmony with my own Mission Statement, I shall be
available for as many activities as are practical to my own schedule.
Large or small, old or young . . . all becomes irrelevant when immersed
in inspirational interdependence!

Name ....

Address ....

....

.... Postcode ....

Telephone ....

Occupation ....

Contribution ....
                    towards seasonal newsletter, meeting costs and general administration

Membership Number ..... *to be allotted* .....

Let's enjoy today, and look forward to a rosy future together.

Phil Murray
Leader of the PAC, 1st January 1997

PAC is an acronym for Positive Attitude Club.
The PAC philosophy states simply that improvement of personal life
through positive attitudes benefits humanity as a whole.
We are an independent non-profit-making organisation dedicated to peaceful
interdependence through creative discussion and forward thinking for the world.